Most Commonly Asked Questions

- Do I vacuum or dust first?

- Is there an easy way to clean and maintain window blinds?

- Can I stop toys and papers from spreading through the house?

- Can I get rid of mildew permanently?

- Is it better to use paper towels or newspaper to clean windows?

- Why does the trim around my self-cleaning oven not get clean after it's been set to clean?

- How can I remove rusty stains from my white counters?

- How do you clean exhaust vent covers and keep them clean?

- How do you keep the woodwork clean and shiny?

- How can I get in touch with you, and will you answer my questions to help me speed up my cleaning process?

You will find answers to all these questions inside this book.

Dear Richard,
Bust the dust, keep it clean!
Jane Lawson

HOUSECLEANING
Jane Lawson's WAY

E**p**ic
Press

Belleville, Ontario, Canada

Housecleaning Jane Lawson's Way

Copyright © 1999, Jane A. Lawson

Canadian Cataloguing in Publication Data

Lawson, Jane (Jane A.)
    Housecleaning Jane Lawson's way

ISBN 1-55306-004-0

    1. House cleaning. I. Title.

TX324.L39 1999   648'.5   C99-900627-4

For more information on how to arrange for a training program, seminar, speech or personal consultation, or to order additional copies, please contact:

Jane Lawson, The Clean Queen™
P.O. Box 4224, Peabody, MA 01961 USA
Tel: (978) 535-7091; Fax: (617) 884-5209
E-mail: queenclean@bigfoot.com

Printed in Canada
by

Epic Press

Dedication

This book is dedicated to those people who inspired me to write it. They are my viewers, listeners, students, and participants of my seminars who constantly kept asking me for more and more detailed information – preferably a book.
It is my husband, Bruce, who has always been helpful and supportive of my work.
I thank you all.

Get Ready For Cleaning

Congratulations! By reading this book, you have just taken the first step to a clean, orderly house, whether you choose to clean it yourself or hire someone to do it for you. You do-it-your-selfers will learn how to work smarter, not harder. Yes, you can cut the time it takes to clean your home in half!

Those of you who are ready to throw in the towel (and mop!) will learn how to hire a professional – what to expect, what to ask for, and how to evaluate that person you're about to let into your home.

We'll set some goals – some reasonable goals – together. Remember, you live in a house, not a museum. (Yes, it's okay to have one little corner where a mess is allowed.)

You'll find that you're spending less time maintaining your residence and more time enjoying it. You'll spend less time looking for lost items. You'll improve your lifestyle.

Let's get started!

Contents

Chapter 1: First Things First **9**

The Grand Tour of Your Home. 11

Schedule 15

Plan of Attack. 18

Proper Clothing. 20

Right Equipment. 21

Quality Supplies. 28

Chapter 2: Step By Step **41**

Before We Begin 43

Kitchen 53

Bathroom. 65

Living Room, Family Room, Den 73

Dining Room 78

A Few Useful Tips. 80

My Top Ten Household Tips 84

Chapter 3: Spring Cleaning **89**

What is Spring Cleaning? 91

Where Do I Start?. 95

Helpful Tips 101

Chapter 4: Still Need Help? Hire a Pro **103**

Determine Your Needs. 105

Per Hour or Per Job 108

Self-Employed or Large Company. 108

Go For It! 115

A Personal Note from the Clean Queen™

Dear reader,

This book gives you practical, current, and tested information on how to cut your cleaning time by as much as 50%. It is the result of 15 years of research, trial and error experience, and hard work in the housecleaning business.

This book is loaded with tips, suggestions, and recommendations for everyone – young mothers and fathers, families with busy schedules, those who do not have enough time to clean, and those who hate housework.

Save thousands of dollars per year on cleaning services. Pamper yourself, take a vacation, put a downpayment on a new car!

Here's my promise to you: **If you don't substantially cut down your cleaning time, you may contact me for a personal phone or mail consultation up to one year after the purchase of this book.**

Jane A. Lawson
The Clean Queen™
P.O. Box 4224
Peabody, MA 01961
Tel: (978) 535-7091; Fax: (617) 884-5209
E-mail: queenclean@bigfoot.com

Chapter 1

First Things First

The Grand Tour of Your Home

Before you start cleaning, you have to evaluate your home to discover how much work lies ahead. To do this crucial step, take a walk around your house and evaluate each area's cleaning needs. With a sheet of lined paper on a clipboard, answer two questions: How much time will it take? How much time am I willing to spend on it?

Some things, like the top of the stove, have to be done every time you clean. Others, like the inside of the kitchen cabinets, don't have to be done that often. Make a list of the **basic** jobs that have to be done each time – for example, the stove top. Then make a second list of those **extra** tasks that can be alternated with one another – for example, polishing silver, cleaning fingerprints of walls. They too have to be cleaned, but less often. Make a third list of things you would love to do but deep down inside you know you'll never do – for example, cleaning your garage or basement. I call this a **wish list**. You might want to save it for spring cleaning, otherwise just throw it away.

Keep your lists *realistic*. Make sure you'll be able to meet your goals when the excitement of a new venture has worn off. There are other things in life to do besides clean!

My list of extras includes things like cleaning the insides of the refrigerator and oven, pulling out the attachments of the vacuum cleaner to get in the corner behind the sofa, and cleaning every little crystal on the chandelier. Your list should include whatever is important to you but which does not need to be done every time you clean.

I always start with the extras, because then I have the most energy and they get done faster, plus I don't mess up a clean house. If I save the extras for the end, I know I'll say to myself, "Let's save that for the next time. I'm out of time and energy now." And one more reason to do it first: It is difficult to estimate how long it will take you to clean this particular extra, because it's so seldom that you do it.

Put everything on paper and commit yourself to the **'basic'** amount of work on a regular schedule. Also list your **'extras'** and mark down the date when each was done last. Make it like a chart, so you can keep track of when it's time to check out the inside of the fridge or the chandelier. I know it seems fanatical, but try it for a while. You'll find that it works, and then you'll be in a rhythm and won't need a written schedule anymore.

It is nearly impossible for me to put together a list of basic, extra, and spring cleaning duties to suit everyone, because our standards and needs are different, our furniture and size of our homes are different, our family size and responsibilities are different. Therefore, the following chart is just a guideline. Feel free to move an extra into the basic column, or vice versa, to suit your needs.

If you find yourself being overwhelmed by extras, lump them all together into one day. It might have to be an additional day every month or two (less then ten times per year). You'll find it much easier to do your basic work if you don't have to do extras every time.

You should put whatever is important to you first on your list.

BEDROOM, LIVING & DINING ROOMS	GARAGE, BASEMENT, ATTIC
BASIC	**BASIC**
Dust/polish furniture	Clean cobwebs
Dust baseboards, mouldings as needed	Sweep/vacuum floor
Sweep, wash or vacuum	Dust/clean furniture & shelves
Clean mirrors	Clean washer/dryer
Clean cobwebs	Empty trash
Empty trash	
Dust blinds	
Dust knickknacks	
EXTRA	**EXTRA**
Dust behind furniture	Wash floors
Clean fingerprints off walls & switchplates	Vacuum furniture
Wax floors if needed	Clean behind washer/dryer
Dust lampshades	Organize laundry supplies
Wash blinds	Sort out stuff that's piled up
Dust walls	
Dust ceiling fan	
Vacuum soft furniture	
Chandeliers	
SPRING	**SPRING**
Wash/oil furniture	Clean behind furniture & boxes
Wash/oil baseboards & mouldings	Oil/wash furniture
Wash behind & under furniture	Get rid of junk!
Window treatments	
Wash walls as needed	

KITCHEN	BATHROOM
BASIC	**BASIC**
Top and outside of stove	Mirrors
Burner plates	Tub
Stove hood	Tile
Counter tops	Shower door
Small appliances	Soap dishes
Refrigerator outside	Toothbrush holder
Microwave – inside & out	Sink
Coffee pot	Cabinet doors – outside
Toaster	Toilet
Cabinet doors – spot clean	Sweep floor
Sweep & wash floors	Dust blinds
Window above sink	
EXTRA	**EXTRA**
Oven – inside	Medicine chest – inside
Vent covers	Light fixtures
Refrigerator – inside	Shower mat
Behind microwave	Runners in shower door
Toaster – inside bottom	Shower curtain
Cabinet doors – inside & out	Cabinet doors – inside
Dust baseboards	Clean/replace brush holder
	Baseboards – spot clean
	Wash windowsills
SPRING	**SPRING**
Drawer under stove	Wash/oil cabinets
Floor under that drawer	Cabinets – inside
Cabinet shelves	Wash/oil baseboards
Behind refrigerator	Windows
Windows – inside & out	

Schedule

You will save yourself hours of labor if you set your schedule **correctly**. Too many people put off housecleaning until they just can't stand the condition the house is in. By that time, you need a shovel, not a dustpan, just for the dirt on the kitchen floor. What a mistake! You've created a physically exhausting monster job that takes all day or an entire weekend. This is a vicious cycle – cleaning becomes such a miserable ordeal that you put it off and put it off, guaranteeing that it will always be a miserable ordeal.

The antidote? Do not let your home reach the 'ordeal' state. Figure out how much time it will take to maintain your home on a bi-weekly or tri-weekly basis. If you live alone and travel half of the month, then once a month might do it for you. Find the schedule that works for you and **stick with it. Don't allow your house to reach the 'Oh my goodness – I'll never get it clean' condition. *You have to clean your home when it is not yet dirty but is definitely not clean anymore.***

For most households, bi-weekly cleaning is adequate. Some homes, especially those with children, require more frequent picking up and straightening out, but actual cleaning of the home seldom is needed weekly.

Occasionally, you should go off schedule if it will save time in the future. If your refrigerator is just about empty and in need of an inside cleaning, do it the evening before you go shopping. It's faster because there's less stuff in it. It gives you the chance to take stock and to see if something has gone bad. Most people shop more often than they need to clean the fridge, so this system works great. Doing it now is much easier than cleaning it when it's full.

If you're giving a bath to your young child, clean the bathroom while she's sitting there splashing. As soon as she's out of the tub, clean that right away too. Now you can pretty much skip the bathroom during your next basic cleaning. Because your child bathes more often than you need to clean the bathroom (I hope), you will not even need to clean it every time you bathe the child. This system will also leave you time to play with your child.

Here are some other scheduling factors to consider. If you live in a small apartment, you have to clean your entire home every time you clean because you use every bit of space. But if you live in a two-storey colonial, chances are your upstairs stays clean longer than your downstairs. Perhaps you can alternate complete upstairs cleaning with just cleaning the upstairs bathrooms. Do you have a den and a spare bedroom that don't see much use? Alternate them. No one will know except you.

Another way to cut time is by alternating areas (like dusting baseboards one time you clean, dusting window blinds the next time).

Items or areas you alternate ideally should take the same amount of time and energy. Another option is to clean your master bedroom every time, but alternate the kids' bedrooms. Unless you have very unusual children, they won't care one bit, and the bedrooms will look good too.

Family cooperation shouldn't have to be scheduled, but probably will have to be enforced. Some families have one or two days appointed each week for picking up and putting away. If every family member cooperates, this doesn't take more than ten or fifteen minutes each time.

With kids, a good rule is, "If any toys are left on the floor around the house after bedtime, they are mine." You can take the toy away for a period of time or give it to charity. Kids learn fast.

A spouse is harder to deal with. You might try to make him or her cooperate but if you are fighting a losing battle, designate an area where complete disorder is allowed and try to confine it to that area. If you cannot win, at least you might succeed in stopping the chaos from spreading!

Never again will a cleaning job wipe you out. You'll have more time and more energy available after you clean. Go dancing or treat yourself to a fancy dinner with the money you saved by doing it yourself! And you'll still have enough energy to really enjoy it.

Plan of Attack

Now that you've made a commitment to clean and you know how often you will do it, you must create your own plan of attack. This will be your plan of actual cleaning – where to start, where to proceed, and where to finish.

If you live in an average size home with 12 areas (counting hallways, back room, pantry, and any other areas in addition to rooms in your home) and you speed up your cleaning process in each area by five minutes, you will save an entire hour!! Can you imagine how much time you can save if you really put some thought into planning your work and using my tips? Amazing! And if you use the cleaning products that are best for your needs, you can easily cut your cleaning time in half.

Know where you'll start, where you'll go next, and where you'll finish. You will be most efficient if you start with the hardest jobs and finish with the easiest. Start on the main level of the house. Clean the kitchen first, and then clean the bathroom on the same level only! Next, do your dusting and polishing, clean glass and mirrors, and finish with the vacuuming. Moving on to the next level, start in the bathroom (assuming you do not have a second kitchen). Follow the same sequence as on the main floor and congratulations – you're done for the next two weeks!

No matter what type of residence you have, go in this order:

- Kitchen
- Bathroom on that level
- Dusting
- Vacuuming

If there's another level below, vacuum your stairs going down, and continue with:

- Bathroom
- Dusting
- Vacuuming on that level

If your next level is up – clean it, vacuum it, then vacuum your way down the stairs. It is much easier to vacuum stairs going down.

Proper Clothing

There are three main considerations regarding clothing for cleaning: comfort, safety, and not worrying about getting them dirty.

Tight blue jeans cut your circulation when you bend down, so you cannot work comfortably and efficiently. Your best choice of clothing is sweatpants or shorts, or even an old swimsuit on a hot summer day. Whatever you wear, make sure it is comfortable. Add to it a sweatshirt or a t-shirt and you are all set.

Sneakers or rubber-soled shoes prevent falls on wet, slippery floors. Do not wear sandals or open-toed shoes. It is easy to hurt bare toes. You should concentrate on working, not worrying about your feet.

Don't wear anything with loose flaps flying around. They could get caught or snagged.

I guarantee that you will stain your clothing sooner or later, so make sure you're not wearing something you might want to wear in front of someone else. If you're worried about clothing, you will slow down. It is a great idea to wear the same outfit every time you clean – it gets your mind in cleaning mode.

Right Equipment

There is only one piece of equipment that is pretty much essential – a vacuum cleaner. If you have hardwood floors, you might want a floor buffer. The only other machine you may want to invest in is a carpet shampooer.

A VACUUM CLEANER is a must in every home regardless of whether or not you clean by yourself or hire help. You need a vacuum cleaner for the in-between times when your child knocks over a houseplant and spills dirt over the carpet or when you need to pick up dog hairs off the floor or furniture.

Decide if you prefer a canister or an upright model. There are advantages and disadvantages to both.

Let's consider the upright first.

An upright is much easier to work with, especially on stairs, because there is only one piece to hold. An upright is a lot easier to use in open areas, again because you don't have to pull the canister along. However, because of the size of the bottom, you might not be able to reach every corner. You have to fuss with attachments. On the other hand, you do not need to reach every corner every time.

Now let's look at the canister. The benefit of a canister is that you do not need to use attachments because the brush at the end of a hose can reach into every corner. However, there are a few problems with a canister. It is very difficult to vacuum stairs because you are using a brush at the end of a hose while the whole body of a canister vacuum cleaner is hanging on the other end. Also, when you concentrate your attention on vacuuming the carpet with a brush at the end of a hose, it is easy to bump the furniture because you are not watching the body of the vacuum cleaner. And if you do watch it, you will lose a lot of time.

I vote for the upright with quick and easy attachments. You should choose what you're comfortable with.

Occasionally, you have to vacuum in a tight corner or under a piece of furniture. In this case, attachments to the vacuum cleaner should be used. If you have a canister, no problem. If you have an upright, you need attachments. The attachments on modern vacuum cleaners come on and off quickly and easily. If you have an older type that uses clips to attach and remove attachments, consider trading it in. You waste time putting the attachments on and taking them off, or else you walk around the house twice to vacuum, once with attachments and once without.

Some uprights are sold with a "free" hand vac for hard to reach areas. That means you have to carry another piece of equipment with you or make an extra trip through the whole house just to get into corners. Either way, it's a nuisance or a waste of time.

Choose an upright with attachments mounted right on the back of the machine. They hook up almost instantly. You pull out the hose that leads to the main brush, and just as quickly insert the hose for the attachment.

Central vacuums are wonderful but expensive. If you have the bucks, go for it.

Some people like the very expensive (over $1,000), commercial quality vacuums. They last forever and are well designed. Some of them even have self-powered wheels. I don't like them. Why would you want a vacuum cleaner to last you a lifetime? There is always something new and better coming on the market. If you have over one thousand dollars invested in a vacuum cleaner, you won't want to put it aside for something new, and it's tough to get a good return if you trade it in. Besides, if you have that much money, you'd be better off investing in a central vacuum cleaner. Some of these vacuum cleaners are very heavy (something I like to avoid) because they are made for life with a lot of metal.

I would buy a new vacuum every few years, for two hundred dollars or so. If each vacuum lasts for five years, which it should without abuse, over a 25-year period, you will spend about $1,500 (allowing for some inflation) on five vacuum cleaners. When you consider the future value of $1,200 against the cost of replacing the vacuum every five years, I think you do better replacing the vacuum. Plus, with each new purchase comes a new one-year warranty.

When it's time to buy a vacuum cleaner, go to a store with a good selection where you can see, touch, try, lift, and get answers to your questions. Then make your decision and buy one. Don't spend more than about $200. If money is a problem, buy a used one. Check your yellow pages for vacuum cleaner repair shops. You will find what you want at half the price, with a warranty. I have bought several used vacuum cleaners (with warranties) for my business with no problems.

Do not get carried away and buy a commercial strength vacuum cleaner, no matter how persuasive that door-to-door salesman is. You do not have commercial traffic in your home and you do not have commercial strength carpet either. Whatever your choice is, a few things are a must:

1. Buy the most powerful home vacuum cleaner you can afford. It should be rated at 12 amps, at least.

2. Attachments should be mounted on the rear of the vacuum and must snap on and off quickly and easily.

3. It must be lightweight and easy to maneuver.

4. Bags should be easily and quickly replaceable, with a minimum of dust escaping during the changing procedure. The quicker you change the bag, the less dust you will breathe in. You should not feel that you are breaking into Fort Knox just to change the bag.

Notes:

1. Remember that as the bag fills, the vacuum cleaner loses power, has less suction, and works harder. It is up to you to decide how full the bag will be before you change it.

2. To prevent attachments from sticking together, lightly coat the ends of each with petroleum jelly.

3. To prevent a retrievable cord from snapping back into the vacuum cleaner if you accidentally tug too much, clip a clothespin to the cord when it is pulled out to the length you want.

4. Attachment brushes are small for two reasons. Smaller brushes have greater suction, and they get into tight corners more easily.

5. Save 20 minutes in an average home (plus save a lot of bending) by plugging in your vacuum cleaner just once in a central location. Use a 25 foot extension cord, and you'll be able to reach all or most of your house. Check with your hardware store that the cord you're purchasing is the right one for your vacuum. Make a knot between the extension cord and the vacuum cleaner cord before attaching them so they will not come apart. If your older home does not have three-pronged grounded sockets, attach an adapter permanently to your most central socket. If you do need the adapter, make sure you ground it properly.

Now you and your vacuum cleaner are ready for a speedy quality job.

If you have allergies to dust or pollen, buy a vacuum cleaner with a hepa filter. Clean the filter periodically. Replace it every year. The cost of the vacuum is between $150 and $280. Filters cost between $20 and $60.

A BUFFER-POLISHER is another piece of equipment you will need if you have a hardwood floor with a satin finish that requires waxing. It is not for use on polyurethane-finished floors. You will need a buffer at least twice a year. It can be rented from many hardware stores or some supermarkets for about $20 per day.

My advice is to buy. You can get a good machine for as low as $150. You won't have the nuisance of lugging it back and forth to the rental store. This is important because a buffer is guaranteed to dirty your car.

A CARPET CLEANER is needed occasionally to shampoo your carpets. Think hard before you buy one. You might need to clean your carpets once a year. Can you commit to cleaning your carpets for years to come? If you're sure you'll still be willing to do it in three or four years, then go ahead and buy one. If you're not sure, then rent it. Beware the warranty on a carpet cleaner. It will probably be for one year, but you only will use it at most once a year, so the warranty is not worth much.

Just like with a vacuum cleaner, there may be improvements coming in a few years that might render the one you buy today obsolete. Please, before you run out and buy a carpet cleaner (even if it is on sale), analyze your needs and your level of commitment. Will it become another piece of clutter?

Remember that if you spill coffee, you can use a carpet stain remover. You do not need to use the shampooer. Besides buying or renting, you might consider hiring someone every two or three years to do it professionally and you will have a very easy job of maintaining your carpet in between, To hire will cost you $25 or $35 per room. Stairs are usually considered as one room.

To rent a carpet cleaner will cost you about $20 for a day. If you prepare your home for shampooing before you rent the machine, there will be plenty of time to finish the job in one day, no matter how big the house is. Make sure you buy enough cleaning solution so you do not run out in the middle of a job.

Quality Supplies

There are countless housecleaning products on the market, and new ones are introduced every week. The trick is to find out which one is best for you. They all will do the job or they would be off the market, but some require vigorous scrubbing and some don't. Some you layer on and wipe off, some you spray on, wait, and then scrub. Do not get overwhelmed. Of course, you can buy one at a time and test them one by one, but that would be costly and time consuming.

I have included a list of my favorite cleaning supplies below, but if you do not care for these, there is another way to find what's best for your needs. Just ask. You can ask people who sell your type of furniture, tile, floor covering... or who manufacture the product, who install... and if all else fails, call every 1-800 number you can get your hands on.

I have tested a lot of cleaning products myself and feel strongly that in general sprays are less effective on tough dirt. They are not as abrasive as scouring powders or liquid-paste cleansers. Brand names usually clean better than imitations. It is better to spend a bit more money and buy a product that works than to save a dime and rub and scrub and lose valuable time and energy.

Don't stock up with an unlimited variety of cleaning solutions. Many cleaners can be used in more than one location around the house.

Do read labels carefully before you buy. The big lettering on the bottle might scream "FLOOR CLEANER" but the small print will say exactly what kind of floor it cleans. Be especially careful with linoleum floors, because there are a few different linoleum finishes. Make sure the cleaner fits your particular need.

Always follow the directions on the container. Let me repeat this. Always follow the directions on the container. Not only will the product clean more effectively, but it will be safer. You will avoid harsh chemicals damaging your skin. You will avoid breathing in dangerous vapors. You will avoid toxic mixtures of chemicals. Be especially careful when disposing of cleaning solutions.

Never mix two cleaning products together, even in disposing them. Bleach and ammonia, for instance, can form chloroform when mixed together. Chloroform can be fatal.

Here's a list of my preferred supplies:

SUDSLESS AMMONIA: Keep a spray bottle full of a 1:4 solution. Use it on glass or plastic. You can change the mix a bit – perhaps a little stronger for the bathroom, milder for the bedroom mirror. Never spray it directly on the mirror (mist is bad for furniture). Spray on a paper towel, then wipe the mirror. When using ammonia, make sure you have adequate ventilation.

WIRELESS TOILET BRUSH: To avoid silver streaks in the toilet after each cleaning, use a wireless toilet brush. The bottom of it fits in the bottom of toilet just right to make your job easy, the top reaches very conveniently under the trim of the toilet, and the handle is very strong.

TOILET CLEANER: Most of them are good. Solutions containing bleach are better for toilets with rust stains, mineral deposits, or older toilets with a worn finish. They contain a SMALL amount of bleach, not enough to destroy the finish, yet enough to clean. Never use straight bleach! It can gradually damage the finish. Never use bleach if you have a septic tank – you will ruin that too.

A PUMICE STONE will get rid of stubborn rust stains, and it will not scratch. A pumice stone (one of the fine ones that are used to remove mineral deposits from the sides of swimming pools, not one for removing corns from your feet) can be picked up at a swimming pool supply store. The drawback to a pumice stone is that it requires time and tedious manual labor to do the job.

Products that you pour and soak don't always work as well, especially on the rusty trim at water level. A surprisingly effective toilet cleaner is a denture cleaning tablet. Just drop one tablet into the toilet, let it dissolve, and clean away the ugly stains with a toilet brush.

CARPET CLEANER: Before buying one, know what your carpet is made of. Some carpet cleaners do not work on or may discolor wool carpets. Avoid cleaners that are good for all kinds of carpet; it's like buying a one-size-fits-all shirt.

FURNITURE POLISH: Any furniture polish is good. I cannot say that one brand is better than the other. Spray some on a piece of cloth and wipe the surface of your furniture. Some people use it too often; this not only slows down the process of cleaning but creates a heavy build-up of wax (with time, of course). Use it only if you need to wipe off fingerprints or stains or to give your furniture an extra shine. For regular dusting, use a dusting spray.

DUSTING SPRAY: Just like furniture polish, no one particular brand is better than the other. This product is similar to furniture polish but has no wax in it, which causes a build-up. It is designed to take dust away. It is best if used with feather dusters.

ELECTRONICS SPRAY is canned air under pressure, sort of like a can of room freshener without the scent. Use it to blow off your computer, VCR, stereo, and other electronic appliances. If you use a feather duster it takes more time and can also push dirt inside if you're not careful.

FEATHER DUSTERS: There is a huge variety of feather dusters on the market today. You have the choice of pretty colors, artificial or natural feathers, wool, and different shapes. Which one is best to buy? I prefer the one that requires the least maintenance, which is the fluffy, feathery type. From the tip of the handle to the end of the feathers it is about 12 inches long. Usually I buy them on sale at a discount store for $1.00. In the supermarket, they cost about $2.00.

I don't like the long, skinny type for general cleaning. Those work best for slots that are hard to reach (like the space between the refrigerator and the wall).

Some of them can be washed, however, by that time they look so pitiful that they should be replaced. And considering the price, replacement is painless. When feather dusters are replaced, use the old ones to sweep hair on the bathroom floor – quick and easy.

Before buying a feather duster, peel the plastic cover back and shake it well. Usually some light fluff will come out. This is OK if it stops after a few seconds. If it keeps on shedding, it is of poor quality and will create more work for you. Put it down and take another one.

I don't think the price of a feather duster is related to how well it works. Ostrich feather dusters are very expensive. I don't think they're worth the cost and time. It's better to use an inexpensive one without maintenance and replace it a few times per year.

Many people do not use feather dusters **properly**. Be sure to see the section on dusting (p. 73) for instructions.

SPONGES: Sponges are easier to grasp and have more absorbent power than cloths. They are also more economical than paper towels.

Always buy cellulose sponges. Don't buy shiny, "plasticky"-looking sponges. They're not absorbent at all. The difference is that you need to go over the surface again with a paper towel if you use a plasticky sponge, using more supplies, time, and energy.

I strongly recommend my 12 + 2 system – six standard and one abrasive sponge for the kitchen, and the same for the bathroom. Six sponges are enough to eliminate constant walking to the sink and back. The abrasive sponge will save time and loosen up dirt with much less physical effort. To clean them, put kitchen sponges in the dishwasher every time you run it or put them in a pot and boil. Bathroom sponges go in the washing machine. Always lay them out to dry. The longer sponges stay wet, the sooner they will deteriorate and need replacement.

To prevent bathroom sponges from ending up in the kitchen sink, mark them by cutting off one small corner from every bathroom sponge. To make sure your **toilet sponges** do not get mixed up with the sink sponges, **cut off two corners** from two sponges for the toilet cleaning only. Don't try to sort them by color. If you run out of one color, you're in trouble.

STEEL WOOL BALLS: I use soapless steel wool only for the stove, burner plates, ovens, and stainless steel sink. Don't buy ones with soap. They're usually overloaded with a mild cleaner that makes a big soapy mess. You scrub harder and it takes longer to clean up all those suds. What a waste of time and energy! With soapless pads, you add the right cleaner and the right amount for the job at hand. Soapy pads are good for cleaning delicate items that can be easily scratched by a harsh, soapless steel wool ball.

PAPER TOWELS should always be of good quality. Cheap paper towels leave lint and don't last. You use so many more of them that you don't end up saving any money. You can use folded towels. They are stronger, don't leave lint, and are cheaper. You can purchase them in wholesale stores.

MILDEW REMOVER: There are many good mildew removers on the market. Make sure it specifically says mildew remover. Generally, **brand names** work better than generic or store brands. For mildew on walls and ceilings, buy mildew-resistant paint in a paint store. They guarantee no mildew for five years.

PITCHER: You need this tool to rinse the tub only if you do not have a flexible shower hose. After the tub or the shower stall is soaped up, the best way to rinse it is with the hose. If your shower does not have a detachable hose, use a **half-gallon** pitcher to do the job. A large pitcher will take a long time to fill up and will be too heavy to lift, and a small pitcher will not hold enough. Splash water on the wall and not only will it be quicker than wiping with a sponge, but you will not have to wipe streaks – there will not be any.

EFFICIENCY BELT: My housecleaning belt does for me what a carpenter's belt does for a carpenter – it keeps all of my small tools at hand. I designed it myself specifically for housecleaning to keep all needed supplies at hand. Load it according to your needs. It frees your hands so you can use both of them to clean, not to carry your bottles. It assures that you do not lose, spill, drop, or forget your bottles anywhere. They are always conveniently next to you. My belt is waterproof so I don't get wet or dirty. It is washable, too. I tried to carry a caddy for tools but I still needed a hand to carry it, I still needed to bend down to put it down and to pick it up – and the worst – my paper towels were getting wet from other cleaners no matter how I tried to protect them.

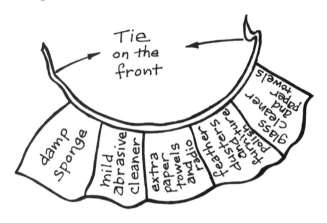

For ordering information, see the form in the back of the book.

BROOM: Any broom is good for home sweeping as long as the bristles are soft. The traditional stiff, corn whisk broom is not recommended for sweeping at home because it sweeps dust into the air. In a minute, the dust settles on surfaces you have just cleaned. This stiff whisk broom is good for outdoor sweeping of sand and leaves from sidewalks, drive-ways, and front steps.

DUST MOP: A terrific tool for cleaning floors and walls. I use two dust mop heads: one for floors and one for walls.

If you have a dust mop handle and need another head, bring the old head with you to the store. There are so many varieties you could easily buy the wrong size. Styles don't differ very much, and I don't think one style is better than another. Buy the cheapest one you can find.

Always spray a dust mop with NO WAX dusting spray before using it. Otherwise, you'll just be pushing dust around. If you use a spray with wax, you will leave the floor slippery.

MOP: I recommend lightweight sponge mops with replaceable heads. String mops are harder to work with. They are heavy when wet and splash water around, leaving dirty spots on the bottom of cabinets you've just cleaned. Any sponge mop with a screw-on replacement head is good, but brand name mops tend to keep their flat shape longer. The handle and head clamp will last a long time but the sponge wears out every few months. Make sure that replacement sponges are available. Avoid pop-in replacement heads because they tend to be poor quality.

FLOOR CLEANERS can damage a surface they're not designed for. Read labels and follow the instructions.

Tile floors – Hardly any cleaner can damage the tiles themselves, but some cleaners can damage grout. Make sure the label mentions tile **floors**. Stay away from tile cleaners suited for wall or counter tiles, and stick with floor tile cleaners.

One of the few products I recommend by name is Color Grout. It colors grout and prevents damage from cleaning products. The grout will remain the same color, even in high traffic areas where you would expect it to blacken. Color Grout is available in floor covering stores.

No wax linoleum floors – The less cleaner you use, the longer a no-wax floor will stay shiny. Every cleaner contains harsh chemicals that will eventually dull the shine of your no-wax linoleum floor. It doesn't happen overnight, and by the time you see the finish getting duller, it is usually too late; the damage is done. To make matters worse, linoleum is a porous material. When the shiny, protective finish is gone, it soaks up dirty wash water like a sponge. When dirty water is absorbed, the linoleum floor looks dirty, and it's impossible to make it look clean. Once you wash it, it will be clean, but it still will not look clean.

Floor covering stores often sell a cleaning product that is designed specifically for no-wax floors. This is the cleaner I prefer. However, even this cleaner should be thoroughly rinsed off.

Hardwood floors – Never wash hardwood floors!!! There are two kinds of finishes on hardwood floors. A polyurethane finish is a coating that protects the floor from damage by water, but water makes it dull. You will have to refinish your floors often if you wash them every time you clean. There is a limit as to how many times floors can be refinished, because every time you refinish, the boards gets thinner and thinner. Don't push it!

The other type of hardwood floor finish is called

satin finish – in this case, there is no protective coat of polyurethane to protect the floor from water. These floors should not be washed because water will get between the boards and ruin the floor. The floor will squeak, turn gray, or even rot.

Satin finish floors should be waxed twice a year, preferably in late spring before summer heat comes in and in late fall before winter heat is turned on. This will minimize the effect of heat drying out the wood.

Some companies try to convince you that their products are safe for washing wood surfaces, including hardwood floors. Don't believe it. Wood and water are not friends – they are big enemies. Any cleaner that you have to use **with a lot of water and a little bit of cleaner** will be bad for your hardwood floor. There are some new products on the market designed to be used **without water or with very little water**. Those are okay, but do not use them every time you clean or you will see a horrible build-up after a while.

The solution? Spot cleaning. When you see a stain that the dust mop doesn't pick up, use a damp sponge to wipe it off.

OIL FOR WOODWORK (other than the floor): Certain types of woodwork such as unpainted doors, door frames, railings, and window frames, and some furniture finishes (especially antique) need to be conditioned twice a year on average to prevent drying out. You need an oil made for that purpose, such as "Lemon Oil" or "Liquid Gold."

AN OVERSIZED TOOTHBRUSH is very useful for scrubbing in tight places. You can use a regular one, but it will take much longer to do the same job. You can buy an oversized one in a novelty or joke shop.

A PLASTIC PUTTY KNIFE can scrape dirt or gum off the floor, counters, or any surface. It is also good for scraping burnt-on drippings from the bottom of the oven. It is a most convenient tool. Just make sure it is plastic not metal, because metal ones will rust, leaving stains, and can scratch easily.

RUBBER GLOVES protect your hands from dirt and germs. I prefer thin surgical gloves. Thick rubber gloves are clumsy and do not have the same feel. They are harder to work with. I do use thick gloves when cleaning the oven or the window blinds for protection from harsh chemicals or cuts. I only use gloves in the bathroom, kitchen, and when cleaning blinds. If you prefer to use gloves all the time, use fabric gloves when dusting; they let skin breathe. If you keep rubber gloves on for two or three hours, your hands will look like wrinkled prunes and will dry and crack. To prevent water from getting inside your gloves, put rubber bands over the gloves just above the wrists. Make sure the bands aren't tight enough to cut off circulation.

PAPER DUST MASK: Use one when you work in a very dusty area. It will protect you from breathing dust into your lungs. It is not a must for a basic cleaning unless you prefer powder cleaners. They are usually effective but, generally, I try to stay away from powders because some of it always gets into my lungs – and it is not exactly a breath of fresh air.

KNEE PADS: Wear knee pads when cleaning – your knees will appreciate it. They will not be dirty or bruised, and you will not be hurt climbing on a hard floor. I don't like a garden pad because you have to carry it. Both your hands need to be free for cleaning. You can get knee pads in a sporting goods store.

As you can see, my list is quite short and that is how it should be. Your goal is to clean the most efficient way, not to collect the most cleaning products on the block. Some people feel really prepared for cleaning when they have a large selection of products at home, but this does not speed up your cleaning process. What is important is that the products you have are best for **your** needs.

Up until now, I have described preparation work. The good part is that you only have to do this once with occasional replenishment. The bad part is that this is only the beginning. Now let's get to the real work.

CHAPTER 2
Step By Step

Before We Begin

In this chapter, you will find a step-by-step description of every detail of home cleaning. Of course, we all clean, and most of us are even happy with our results, but doing a quality job in a speedy way is a trick that you will learn in this chapter. Let me lead you through your home, step by step, room by room, till all is done, in half the time.

Where do you start? Always start with the hardest job (probably the kitchen) or the extra project if you have one for today. In order to succeed in speedy cleaning, you should not include an extra project for a while until you are comfortable with your routine and your timing. Then you may add the extra project to your basic cleaning; otherwise, it might become overwhelming and you might not see a huge time saving which I would very much like you to see. Also try to avoid extra projects **every** time you clean. Do them only occasionally. After a while, you will know how many extra projects you have and how often you need to do them, and it will become easier to plan ahead. At the beginning, you might want to pick a day to clean extras only, just to get it over with.

If you choose to do an extra, my advice is to do it first. One reason is because you do not know how long it will take you to do it, and secondly, when you finish your extra project, you will tend to speed up your basic cleaning to still finish at the usual time. Of course, if you create a monster of a project, you will never finish the extra or the basic. Do the extra first and be reasonable with how big a job you choose for the extra. You are not superhuman, even if you are a parent, a chauffeur, a cook... in addition to your full-time job outside the home.

Remember the list of extra cleaning? Now is a good time to enter the date when you cleaned the refrigerator or the oven or the chandelier. This list also gives you a pretty good idea of when you will have to do it again. Keep this list out of view so that you are not faced with it every day, but in a place where you can find it easily (do not forget that it exists).

A few general tips before we start:

1. Get in the mood. Ask yourself: "How much quicker will I clean my home today compared to my last cleaning?" This is a totally different attitude than: "Will I finish cleaning my home this time in one day?"

2. When you clean, make sure your mind is a bit ahead of your actions so you do not have to stop and waste any time thinking: "What should I do next?"

3. Repetition is great for speeding you up. I'm sure you know this but probably never thought that it can be useful in housecleaning. No matter what you do, if you do the same work again and again, you do it faster and faster no matter how much or how little you try. It's like typing, driving, balancing your check book, or juggling your home, kids, work.... Of course, if your plan

is not working the way you think it should, by all means go ahead and change your routine. But I recommend that you stick to this new improved plan for a while to give it a chance to work. Within a short period of time, you will find the best way that works for you. It does not matter by how much you speed up your cleaning; more important is the fact that you **do** speed up the process of cleaning. Eventually, you will reach your perfect timing that you are happy with.

4. Do not get distracted. This means no watering plants, no changing sheets (you may change them the night before), no answering the phone (you may listen for who is calling in case of emergency), no laundry (you cannot even imagine how much time and energy this takes. First it takes time to sort your laundry, then load the washing machine, then put the wet clothing in the dryer, then pull it out on time not to over dry, then hang it on hangers, then because you are cleaning bring it to the closet. Now multiply that by the number of loads you do. Trust me, it takes a lot more time and energy than you think. Or do not trust me and experiment yourself.) Without a doubt, it always takes longer if you stop and go than if you clean non-stop.

If you need to cut time on laundry, you may put a load of sheets or towels (something that does not require any care) before you start cleaning. And after you are totally done with cleaning, put that load in the dryer and a new load in the wash. This way, laundry will not slow you down and you will save some time too. If you must, put another load in after you finish the first floor and before you go up to clean the second floor.

5. **Do** use two hands as much as possible. You will do quite well if you move both hands the same way. You should not try to do a circular motion with one hand and a square motion with the other. It will not work for most of us. You will save quite a bit of time if you use two hands. Remember my calculations? In an average home (about 12 areas), if you save 5 minutes on each area, you will save an hour of cleaning time! Two hands will help you save more than 5 minutes in each room. It might take some time to get used to, but it will definitely pay off.

6. Minimize moving things. Unplug the toaster and the can opener for safety reasons, but do not carry them to any other place for more convenient cleaning, leaving a trace of bread crumbs. Do not waste time walking from the counter to the table, and don't make a mess of the table while cleaning a toaster, creating even more work for yourself. Simply move the toaster a foot or two. Clean it on the area you did not clean yet and move it back after that part of the counter it was on is cleaned.

7. TV is acceptable when sorting papers but is terrible when you clean. When you deal with papers you are in one place, but when you clean you are all over the house, if you are serious about it. My opinion is that you should take housecleaning seriously, otherwise you will not be able to plan it correctly and stick with your "Plan of Attack" efficiently. If your goal is to get through housecleaning as fast as possible, you need to concentrate on work. It is hard to do if you listen to the radio or even worse if you keep an eye on the TV.

People often think that if they listen to music and move with the beat, they are moving faster. NO! Radio is a total distraction of your focus. These people are much slower in cleaning; it only feels quicker because they move their bodies more. Aerobics does not clean your home, it only exercises your body. Sorry to disappoint you! These people will get more exercise than you, but is this your goal? If yes, that's great; if no, stick to the original plan.

If you feel that you will never get through cleaning without music or some kind of distraction, try it with the radio for a while, then gradually cut down on entertainment. You will see that you can survive without it for two or three hours and you will be much more efficient. This will be a great incentive. Use the efficiency belt if you absolutely must have a radio. A back pocket in the "efficiency belt" is a great place to put a little portable radio. This way you will not get it wet, you do not need a hand to carry it, and it goes where you go. Your neighbors will appreciate it, too, if you do not have to put the stereo downstairs on full blast because you are cleaning the upstairs bathroom and can't hear it.

I know that some of you have to watch or at least listen to soap operas. I can sympathize – so tape them. It will take you half the time to watch if you speed up through the commercials.

8. Always use the least amount of cleaning product possible. It will save you some money, but more importantly, it will take less time to wipe up the excess. It is always quicker to add more cleaner if you need it than to take the excess off. Anyway, after a couple of cleanings, you will learn how much cleaning product you need for a particular job. You need enough cleaning product to loosen up the dirt. That's all, and there is no need to waste your precious time putting on and wiping off excess cleaning product.

9. If you are happy with two or three products for the same job, always use the mildest. You might think a stronger product works wonders, but chances are it will damage your finish more quickly than a milder one. Use the milder product assuming that it **works**. If it does not work, it does not matter how mild it is, it will take too much of your time and energy to use it.

10. Always spray feather dusters before using. This way they will attract dust and keep it, not spread it around. You will know it works because your feather dusters will look dirtier and dirtier after every cleaning. Eventually, they will need replacement. However, old ones can be used to sweep the bathroom floor if you have hair on it. Make sure the floor is very dry. Then just sweep the floor, reaching behind the toilet and behind the door where lumps of dirt accumulate. Shake feather dusters out over a waste basket after use. You might want to hang them on a nail in the corner somewhere out of view.

11. When you are cleaning anything using a wiping motion – i.e. washing a shower stall in the bathroom, polishing furniture, wiping a counter, washing a glass table or sliding door – always wipe from side to side or up and down. Try to avoid cleaning in a circular motion because that will be much slower. Wiping in a circle will make you go over the same area twice, slowing you down by as much as 50 percent. In some cases, **you** might choose to go over a surface twice or even three times, but it should be **your** choice.

12. Always keep the same number of trash bags at the bottom of each waste basket, so that when you take trash out, you can put a fresh bag back in right then and there without having to bring one. And because you have the same

amount of bags in each waste basket, you will bring a new batch only once every 4-6 weeks (they will be used up all at the same time). Do not put a trash bin back after you empty it until after you vacuum the area, because this way you avoid moving it twice. Saves you energy, time, and a lot of walking around. Optional: You do not need to empty the trash when cleaning if your trash day is once a week – take it out once a week only. Do not apply this system to the kitchen garbage can because if trash leaks it will ruin all bags at the bottom. To prevent the kitchen trash bin from getting dirty from leaking bags, it is a good idea to put a double bag in it. However, when it is time to replace the bag, take only one out. The second one will always be there just for protection.

13. Always work in sections. This means that you visually take a section from top to bottom and do not leave that spot until it is totally finished. This way you will be most productive. It also requires planning ahead. Bring everything you need in the pockets of your efficiency belt to eliminate extra trips. When one section is finished, take the next section right next to it, thus moving in a circle around the room and ending where you started. You will not have to stop and think if you missed anything. With this system, it is impossible to miss something. Also, you can easily see how far you have gone within a particular period of time.

14. Always clean from top to bottom. Cleaning the top will cause dust and drips to fall down, so do not create double work. Start on top.

15. When cleaning mirrors, always spray the paper towel not the mirror, because the mist from the glass cleaner will settle on furniture and damage the finish (not right away, but with time, and then it will be too late to do anything about it). On mirrors covered with toothpaste spots, use the wet sponge first to remove stains. Then one wipe with the paper towel with glass cleaner sprayed on it will do the best to speed up the process. If stains are clear on the mirror, they are probably caused by hair spray or perfume – these should be wiped with a cotton ball dipped in alcohol first, then with window cleaner and a paper towel.

16. Keep papers (all incoming mail) in an attractive bin or basket. Have a rule at home – the bin should always have enough room for tomorrow's mail to fit, even if you have to go through a few envelopes each day. Avoid putting catalogs or magazines under the bin. This is a warning – papers begin to spread. Every time you receive a new catalog, the old one should be thrown out. If there is something you need in an old catalog, order it or tear the page out and stick it in the new catalog. Then get rid of the old one. Magazines are a different story. They go in a magazine rack. If you cannot keep up

with reading them, do not renew the subscription. At some point, you will catch up, then renew. In the meantime, keep your eyes open for a coupon to save a bundle when the time comes to renew the subscription. If there are articles you would like to save, put them in files (kids, garden, health, computer...). This way, your counter will always stay neat and clean, and on cleaning days it will be a breeze to clean. You will enjoy it every day too, not only on cleaning day.

A good time to go through the papers in the bin is when watching TV. You sit in one place, you have room to spread out your papers and sort them by piles (bills, articles to keep...). Then work on reducing each pile.

17. After sweeping the floor, spray the toilet seat, the toilet outside, and the floor around the toilet with disinfectant spray and let it sit. When the time comes to clean the toilet, you will not even need a cleaner – just wipe it down. Quick and easy.

Kitchen

Using the same general principle, start with the heaviest jobs in the kitchen – most likely, the stove. Take everything off it (salt and pepper shaker, spoon rest, the tea kettle, etc.) and put them on the counter or the table nearest the stove. Now take all four burner plates to the sink and clean them. Use an abrasive cleaner and soapless steel wool ball (tear off a piece the size you need; do not wet the whole steel wool ball because it will rust before you need to use it again). If that does an adequate job, great; if not, spray the burner plates with oven cleaner and let them sit in the sink while you finish cleaning the rest of the stove. If you prefer, you can consider other options:

1. Replace old burner plates with new ones and keep them clean. This will not be difficult because new burner plates have a finish on them which prevents dirt from sticking. It will also give you an incentive to keep them clean.

2. Buy tin foil covers the size and shape of your burner plates. They are very easy to clean, and you will not have to replace them too often.

3. Cover your burner plates with tin foil. Then you will only have to replace the foil when cleaning. No scrubbing involved at all.

After the burner plates are cleaned (this is where the efficiency belt comes in handy), bring them to the stove, along with six cello sponges, one scrubby sponge, a piece of steel wool, an abrasive cleaner, paper towels, and a glass cleaner. Use a steel wool ball with a bit of abrasive cleaner on it to loosen up stubborn, burned-on dirt. Doing it any other way will take too much effort and energy.

Do not use steel wool all the time on the surface of the stove because it will damage the finish in the long run. To be sure that steel wool is safe to use on your stove, test it first on a small area, or call the stove's manufacturer. When all stubborn dirt is loose, use the scrubby sponge with a cleaner to clean or loosen the spots, grease, and stains. The dirt will still all be there but now it's loose and can be wiped off without any scrubbing. Take two sponges, put them next to each other in the furthest corner of the stove (right or left) and wipe towards yourself. When the sponges get dirty, flip them over. When both sides are dirty, put those two sponges aside and take two clean ones. Because you have six sponges, you'll be able to clean the top of the stove without going to the sink to wash them – a real time-saver.

When you are done with the top of the stove, use paper towels and ammonia to clean the oven door, and then the shiny handle of the oven. Do not forget the drawer at the bottom under the oven; you do not need to empty it every time you clean (put it on the list of extra projects), but always wipe the handle.

Do not forget to wipe the control panel either. If it is painted, do not use anything abrasive or you will take the finish off – guaranteed. If it is a glass panel, do not spray cleaner directly on it or else the cleaner will get behind the glass and you will not be able to get it out. Imagine having to look at it every time you use the stove. Always spray the cleaner on a paper towel then wipe the panel clean.

Wipe under the hood every time you fry something. If greasy stains stay for a week or longer, they are very difficult to remove. It will save you a lot of time and energy later if you wipe grease immediately after frying, even if you do a lousy job. Vent covers should be put in the dishwasher every week, and sponges even more often.

Now that the stove is clean, go back to the sink. If you sprayed the burner plates with oven cleaner earlier, finish cleaning them now. Bring the burner plates and all your sponges back to where you left off. Put burner plates back where they belong, and return the salt and pepper shaker, spoon rest, etc., to their places on the stove. Congratulations, the hardest part of kitchen cleaning is done!

Let's move on to the section next to the stove. You have before you two cabinets on top, two cabinets below, a counter, and maybe an appliance. Use two hands, one holding a soapy sponge and the other a clean, damp sponge. Wipe dirt, drips, spills, fingerprints, etc. from the cabinet door.

Make sure the cleaner you use is right for the surface you are cleaning. Although most cleaners are safe for most surfaces, you must be extremely careful with wood cleaners. Wooden cabinets can have a lot of different finishes. Make sure you get the right cleaner for your finish! When cleaning cabinets, only wipe dirty areas. Cleaning cabinets from top to bottom every time is not needed and wastes time. (Save it for a list of extra projects, when you can clean the whole cabinet, including the inside of the door.)

Now that the cabinets are clean, wipe the counter. If you have a rusty stain from a tuna can or a grape juice spill, use a cleaner with bleach in it. It will do the job without your scrubbing. Save your energy; you still have the whole house to clean. If you have an appliance, move it a foot or two to the side in the direction you are cleaning (so it will not get in your way). Clean it there on a not-yet-cleaned area, then move it back where it belongs. Always unplug an appliance before cleaning it.

Now move on to the section next to where you are. Work again from top to bottom. Eventually, you will make a complete circle around the kitchen and end up where you started. There is no way you will miss anything.

Next wash the floor. First sweep it. If you find a piece of gum or candy stuck to the floor, scrape it off with your plastic putty knife. Fill your bucket with warm water, then add cleaner according to the label. If you add cleaner first and then add water, you will have too many suds.

Wash part of the floor. If a chair is in the way, move it two feet to the side before you wash that part of the floor, and then put it back after you rinse it. When the water gets dirty change it. Use clean water to rinse soap from the floor you just washed, then add more cleaner to it and wash the next part of the floor. Repeat till completely finished.

Remember that linoleum is porous. If you put dirty water on it, it will absorb it and make your floor look old. Have you ever seen an old linoleum floor? It always looks dirty even when it has just been washed. Some of it is caused by wear and tear, but primarily it happens because dirty water gets absorbed by the linoleum every time you wash it. To prolong the life of your floor, keep the water in your bucket clear at all times. If it is not clear, you are putting dirty water on the floor. Dirt works like sandpaper, rubbing the finish and wearing it out more quickly. Use a mop as much as possible. Use a rag to reach where the mop can't.

Avoid moving furniture. Lift one leg of a table, wash under it with a rag, put it down, and lift another one. Or, if the bottom of the table has a stand and is crossed at the bottom, you have two choices: either move the table or use a rag to reach under.

If you have an older linoleum floor and want to shine it up, you might want to use a wax (for linoleum floors only). If you do use wax, try not to wash your floors too often, because every time you wash the floor your wax will lose its shine. Try to sweep only. It might not be a big deal for you to rewax it every week, but wax builds up, creating an ugly, dirty look. Of course, you can buy a stripper for linoleum wax floors (they sell everything you might ever need) but try to avoid extra work and aggravation. It might take much more effort to strip wax and sometimes it still does not come out. This is a big problem because to hire a pro to do it will cost you a fortune. Yes, they are very expensive. My advice – avoid waxes as much as possible.

A Few Tips for the Kitchen

MICROWAVE – To keep it clean, always cover your food with plastic wrap before putting it in to heat. I do not advise that you buy covers, because they create more clutter for your home and you have to wash them every time you use them, so you might as well wash the microwave oven. Plastic wrap is much more convenient for this purpose. When you must clean inside the microwave, fortunately there is an easy way. Put a full cup of water in the microwave (uncovered) and set the timer on high for five minutes. Let the water boil and spill over. Let it sit for a few minutes before opening. Take the cup out and simply wipe. All of the food will still be on the walls of the microwave, but it will be loose so you can just wipe it off without much effort. The bottom glass plate on which you put food in the microwave can be put in the dishwasher or under hot water in the sink for easy clean up.

By the way, when I say wait a few minutes, I do not mean sit down, wait and relax. I mean do something else in the kitchen (keep going in the circle around the kitchen; continue what you were doing before).

REFRIGERATOR – To speed up cleaning the refrigerator, you will need a large trash bag (not a newspaper because it leaves a print on the floor and then you will need to clean that afterwards), six clean, damp sponges, and a scrubby one with a bit of cleaner on it. You might also need a plastic putty knife if there is dried-out food on the bottom of the refrigerator to scrape.

Outside: Pull the chair to the refrigerator and climb on it so you can see and reach everything on top of the refrigerator. Now move everything on top to one side. (If there are too many things, put your right hand at the edge on the right side to keep anything from falling off. With your left hand, clear half of the top of the refrigerator – or at least a third.) Clean it. Then move everything to the left side, wiping each object before you put it down on the clean surface. Now the right side is clear. Clean it. If there is no room to maneuver, take the biggest jar or box and put it on the chair you're standing on. Not only will it make room, but it's also less work to take down one huge jar than a few small ones. Again, by using the six sponges, you should not need to leave your working spot until you're finished.

When the top is done, get down and clean the front refrigerator doors. If the doors are covered with magnets and kids' creations, here is what you do: Starting from the top door, take off all the fancy magnets (only ones that can break if dropped, like ceramic or wood). Stick them on the side of the refrigerator or on the lower refrigerator door. Now, just grab everything else and pull it down. What falls, falls – it's OK; what is hanging at the bottom of the freezer door will hang. Now that you have cleared up most of the freezer door, clean it. Then pull up what is hanging and clean the bottom part of the freezer door. Repeat with the lower door. When you have finished, pick up all that fell. Now stand up and go to the next project. This way you have to bend down only once. Isn't it great?!

Inside: You will not need a chair but will need a trash bag. Clean all your sponges (six plus a scrubby one). Lay a garbage bag on the floor before the refrigerator. Open the fridge and pull the bottom bins out. Put their contents on top of the bag. Look at the bottom of the refrigerator. Does it need soaking? Bring bins to the sink. Fill with the hottest water you can from the faucet – do not use boiling water because it will crack the bin. Hot water with a touch of dishwasher liquid will do the cleaning for you without scrubbing. Leave bins to soak while you clean the rest of the refrigerator.

If you need to soak the bottom of the refrigerator (remember you looked to see?), bring sponges as wet and as hot as possible back to the refrigerator. Squeeze them out to cover the whole bottom that needs soaking with water.

Now start from the top. Take food off the top shelf and put it on the trash bag. Take the shelf out, clean it, put it back, and put food from the second shelf on it. Clean the second shelf, put food from the third shelf on it... get the idea? When you get to the bottom, soak up as much of the water as possible, and go to the sink. Clean all your sponges and the bins and return to the fridge. Put fruit and vegetables (whatever is still edible) back into the bins. Clean the bottom of the fridge with the scrubby sponge and a bit of dishwashing cleaner. Because of previous soaking, you probably will not need to scrub much, but if you do, use a plastic putty knife.

Now put bins into the fridge and clean the door. Take bottles and jars and whatever else you have off the top door shelf. (You'll clean fallen drips off lower shelves as you work your way down.) Clean it. You may bring jars from the lower shelf onto the clean one (always wipe the bottom of the jar before putting it down, otherwise it will leave a dirty stain on the shelf) or put back ones you took out. When the door is done, your refrigerator will look like new and in a very short time. Now wrap all the leftovers and feed the trash. Done!

OVEN – There are a couple of things to know about cleaning inside ovens before you start.

1. It is not as tough of a job as people make it out to be if you know how to do it.

2. Always use gloves because oven cleaners are strong and may damage your hands.

3. Always spray the oven with the cleaner at least an hour before cleaning (be sure to follow directions).

4. Never use oven cleaner or any other cleaner if your oven is self-cleaning or continuous-cleaning. These ovens have a special finish that

permits them to burn stains off. If you scrub the finish, you will damage it and your oven will no longer be self-cleaning.

You must manually clean the outer border around the gasket on the oven door. Also manually clean the corresponding area on the oven itself. Be careful not to damage the gasket. You may use any cleaner you want, but make sure it is totally wiped or rinsed away before you set the oven to clean. You see, the outer part of the oven heats up hot enough to burn the dirt off inside but not hot enough to burn it off the outer part of the gasket, which leaves permanent brown spots. No matter how hard you try to clean it afterwards, it will never look good. The damage is done.

Now let's clean the oven manually. Spray it with oven cleaner and let it sit at least one hour. To protect your floor from drips, spread a plastic garbage bag. I prefer a bag to a newspaper because it will not leave a copy of yesterday's news on the floor, nor will it soak through. Wear heavy rubber gloves. If there is a charred lump, such as burned drippings from an apple pie, scrape it first with a plastic putty knife. Plastic won't scratch or rust. Scrape as much as possible, then use a large piece of steel wool, big enough so you have a good-sized hunk to hold on to. Put some abrasive cleaner on it and get to work. It should not be too difficult to clean your oven at this point. To wipe the loose dirt and cleaner from the oven, I usually use kitchen sponges and then replace them with new ones. (Unfortunately, after you use sponges for the oven they are not usable for anything else). If you need to get rid of the smell from oven cleaner, just bake some orange pieces or peels for about 10 minutes.

TIP – A good way to keep your oven clean is to sprinkle salt on any spills as soon as possible after baking. Let the oven cool, then wipe with a wet sponge. Your oven will always look clean.

DISHDRYING RACK – Whiten it with a cleaner containing bleach. Put a generous amount on the dishdrying rack in the sink and let it sit awhile. Meanwhile, proceed with your cleaning.

DISHWASHER – To remove stains inside, use a generous amount of baking soda (fill both detergent cups). Run the empty dishwasher through a cycle. Or use the same amount of laundry bleach. Skip drying. Wipe outside trim.

TOASTER OVEN – To clean the glass door and/or the bottom that collects bread crumbs, use abrasive cleaner with steel wool. It will not scratch the glass.

MIXER, BLENDER, OR FOOD PROCESSOR – Immediately after use, put in a drop of dishwashing detergent, blend, empty, rinse, fill with water and blend again. Done!

ELECTRIC CAN OPENER – To remove dirt from the blade use a stiff toothbrush.

GARBAGE DISPOSAL – To keep it smelling good, run through citrus peels or (after cleaning the refrigerator) rotten lemons or oranges. Smells so fresh!

VENT COVERS ABOVE THE STOVE – Put them in the dishwasher when needed. If yours look especially dirty, you might have to put them though the wash twice, then keep them clean by washing more frequently.

CABINETS – Clean only stains, fingerprints, and spills on cabinets every time you clean. As an extra, clean the whole cabinet door from top to bottom and do not forget the inside of the door. The whole door does not need to be washed every time, and it will eliminate a lot of unnecessary work for you, speeding up the cleaning process. Hold a soapy sponge in your right hand and soap up the stains. Then with a clean, damp sponge, wipe with the other hand. First the top doors, then bottom doors, then counter space, then the next section. Keep moving. Do not stop!

CHINA – To clean coffee or nicotine stains off china dishes or cups, rub them with a sponge dipped into baking soda.

SMELL

1. To get rid of a smell in a plastic container, fill it with a crumbled newspaper. Cover tight and leave overnight. The newspaper will absorb the smell and it will be gone.

2. To get rid of a fish smell from a cutting board, rub it with a piece of lemon or put some baking soda on a wet sponge and rub the board.

3. To get rid of tomato sauce stains on a plastic container, wash with soap as usual and then

put it out in the sun for a day. Stains will disappear.

AND A COUPLE MORE

To get rid of ugly build-up at the bottom of a vase, add a little bit of dishwashing detergent and hot water and leave overnight. If that does not work well enough, use more detergent and hot water, add crumpled pieces of tinfoil, and shake vigorously.

To prevent dust from sticking to your dust pan, simply wax it. The dirt will not stick!

Here you have a spotless kitchen in about 30 minutes. Done for two weeks! Does this not feel great?!

Bathroom

Using the same system, plan your cleaning of the bathroom. First, while everything is still dry, sweep all hair from the floor (wet hair sticks and can't be swept easily). You can use a broom but often it is difficult to use in a small bathroom. It often does not reach into the corners, which collect the most dirt. You can use a vacuum cleaner but I do not particularly like the thought of using the same brush throughout the house, and it takes more time than you think to hook it up, use it, and unhook it. The better choice is a feather duster. I often use ones that were previously used on furniture and now are replaced by new ones. Use two old ones. When all is swept, they will look pretty dirty. Shake them and rub them against each other over a waste basket to get the dirt and hair out of them.

Now as quickly as possible dump water from a bucket into the toilet (water from washing the floor in the kitchen). This will cause water to drain and the toilet will not fill up again. If you pour the water slowly, the water will not drain completely. Next, squirt your toilet cleaner into the toilet bowl, and it will not be diluted with water. Full strength will have a more powerful effect.

Now spray a disinfectant on the toilet's outside, the trim, the seat (under and over), the lid, the space between the toilet and the tank, and even the floor around the toilet. Let sit for about ten minutes to let the disinfectant work.

But remember the rule – do not rest yet. Clean the tub. Start with the glass doors. Step inside the tub. You may take your shoes off, but it will take time. Put a towel on the bottom of the tub to step on, if you wish; my choice is to stand on two pieces of paper towels (of course, then I do not move because the towel can tear). Make sure you are prepared – you need to have with you one scrubby sponge, some abrasive cleaner, and six sponges. Soap up both glass sliding doors with a scrubby sponge and some abrasive cleaner. First wipe down the door you won't be able to reach once you step out of the tub. Wipe the soap using two hands with a sponge in each hand (just as you did the top of the stove in the kitchen). Now step out of the tub.

If you have a shower curtain, just put it in a washing machine at least once a month, before that white layer of soap scum appears on the inside. If your shower curtain is beyond the cleaning stage, replace it – really – because if you keep the new one clean it will last you forever. Even a broken loop isn't a problem. Just cover it with a heavy duty clear tape or duct tape and punch a hole with a hole puncher. Looks like new.

Let's get back to the tub. If your shower has a hose, great. It is very easy to rinse the other glass sliding door and wet the rest of the tub (you need to wet it before putting any kind of abrasive cleaner on walls and the tub itself or it will be much harder to rinse the cleaner off). Now use your scrubby sponge with abrasive cleaner to soap up the tub, tile, or fiberglass. Make sure your hands are moving up and down or side to side. Remember, you work faster and spend less energy when you do not work in circular motions.

Now rinse, using the hose from a shower if you have one. If you don't, don't worry. Use a medium-sized pitcher, not too big or it will take too long to fill and will be too heavy to lift. Close the glass sliding door all the way to the wall. Splash water on the side tile wall, then on one side of the wall next to it. Move the glass sliding door to the other side and repeat the same. If you have a shower curtain, put two sponges at the edge of the tub wall and a rag on the floor to catch spills. Do not splash water on the wall. Hold the pitcher one half inch from the wall, gently tip, and move from side to side. Water will wash away the soap scum. It will work like a waterfall, and you will be able to control it easily. This works well on side walls. On the back wall where you can't reach, you must splash water on the wall but be careful. When splashing (assuming there is no window), make sure water hits the wall on the way down. If water hits the wall on the way up it will splash all over, creating a mess. So practice!

You might get wet once or twice, but don't panic; you will learn fast. It does not take a genius to figure it out! Now the water will drain, and, believe it or not, the tub does not need you to stand over it and watch. Leave it alone for now. Sorry, still no break time. Look into the toilet. It can be cleaned now; it has set long enough. Use the toilet brush to clean and leave it in. Flush. Look in the tub. Is it OK? If yes – leave it. If no, wipe with sponges whatever settled at the bottom, and open faucets to fill up a bit for the final rinse. Shut the faucets, rinse, drain, and put the shampoo, soap, brushes, or whatever else back, and leave it for two weeks.

Come back to your toilet. Scrub the inside with your toilet brush. Take the brush out and consider it done. To clean the outside of the toilet, use two sponges (with two cut corners, remember?). Close the toilet seat cover. Take the tissue box or whatever you have sitting on the tank lid and put it on top of the toilet seat cover. This way you won't have to leave your working place. Wipe down the tank and its lid. Put back all that you took off, wiping each item first. Wipe down the toilet seat cover on both sides, then the toilet seat itself, wiping the top first, then the bottom.

Next, the outside surface. Remember you sprayed it? So now you do not need to use any cleaner, just wipe. This order is best because as your sponges get dirtier they are used for dirtier areas. As you wipe the toilet outside on the right side, wash that part of the floor beside it. When you wipe the toilet outside on the left side from the top down, wash the floor on that side. You must plan your work beforehand so you have a wet, clean rag to use at the time you need to wash the floor. You will not save any time if, while cleaning the toilet, you leave your place of work to go get the rag, wash it, and get ready.

Now wash one more area that collects dirt. It is behind the door. Wash the rag and the mop (if you use a mop in your bathroom). They are ready for you to use when you need them but not yet. Clean the mirror first. If there are toothpaste stains, wipe it with a wet sponge first, then with a glass cleaner. It will be much faster and you will save energy.

Now the sink. Start from the top – the toothbrush holder. Use a baby toothbrush (keep it there permanently) to clean inside the hole or thread a piece of paper towel through the hole to clean. Do not take all toothbrushes out at once. Take out just one at a time. Put one toothbrush back and then take another out until every hole is cleaned. Soak soap dishes in a sink full of hot water. All the soap will melt. No work on your part at all! If the soap dish is mounted on the wall, put a very wet and very hot sponge on it. In a few minutes you will be able to wipe the melted soap off. No scrubbing!

Cleaning the sink will be next. Use an abrasive cleaner to soap up all of the sink, the surrounding area, and the faucets. Put one sponge on each side of the faucet fixture and pour water on the fixture. Sponges will stop water from spreading. Now with two hands and two sponges wipe area around the sink, then the sink itself.

NOTE: If you pour water on the faucet or any chrome surface to rinse the soap off, it will not leave streaks. But if you wipe it with a sponge, it will leave streaks and you will create double the work by having to wipe it off with a paper towel.

Now having your rag and mop ready (remember you washed them before?), wash the bathroom floor. Done!

Do not put area rugs back yet for two reasons :

1. Let the floor dry. You do not want to keep moisture trapped under the rugs.

2. You need to vacuum rugs. The most efficient way is to vacuum them when the time comes to vacuum the part of the floor right outside the bathroom. By that time, the bathroom floor will be dry and you can put area rugs back.

A few important tips:

1. Toilet – To remove toilet rings, flush first to wet the inside of it. Apply a paste made of borax and lemon juice. Let sit for about two hours, then scrub with a scrubby sponge.

2. If you are like most people and do not like to clean the toilet brush holder, the good news is you do not have to. Throw the holder away as

soon as it is disgusting and replace it with an empty plastic food container, like the size that holds a quart of ricotta cheese. When it gets dirty, just replace it. Your kids might decorate it with stickers. When I had children in diapers, I used the round containers that baby wipes come in. They're more colorful than the ricotta containers. Ask your neighbor or a friend for one if you are through with diapers.

3. If your shower door is all white from soap scum, there is a quick and easy way to clean it. First, make sure that the door is totally dry. Take a large steel wool ball (soapless) and scrub the whole door with it. Everything should be completely dry – the door and the steel wool ball. Use absolutely no cleaner. The soap scum will crumble like chalk. Very fast and very easy!

4. To make your bathroom smell nice, put a drop of your favorite perfume on the light bulb.

5. To clean light bulbs above the sink, make sure the lights are off and not hot. (Hot bulbs can pop when you touch them). Take them out of the sockets. Using soap, wash them, then dry thoroughly and screw back in. You might want to clean the fixture while it is accessible. Spray a window cleaner on a paper towel and wipe. Make sure that moisture does not get inside the fixture. If that does happen, use a hairdryer to dry it before screwing the bulb back. Never spray on the fixture – always on paper towel –

because mist will get inside the electrical part of the fixture!

6. You can save time by not wiping dry the counter area next to the sink. However, metal cans from hair spray or shaving cream may leave rusty stains. To prevent them, put a sheet of toilet tissue under each can. When the counter is dry, throw the tissue out. Or you can paint the bottom of metal cans with clear nail polish before use. Put upside-down to dry. No more rusty rings.

7. If your shower glass sliding doors are clear, use horizontal strokes for one side and vertical on the other side. This way you will easily be able to tell which side still needs cleaning.

8. To clean sliding door tracks, use an oversized toothbrush dipped in a cleaning solution. You may purchase one in a joke shop or a souvenir shop.

9. Wax a curtain rod with a candle to make your shower curtain slide easily.

10. If your bath tub is turning yellow from hard water, cover it with paper towels soaked in vinegar. Let sit for at least two hours. Or, instead of vinegar, use a mixture of automatic dishwashing detergent and very hot water (the hottest possible). Let the towels sit in the tub until they cool enough that you can handle them, then wash away with a scrubby sponge.

Living Room, Family Room, Den...

Just as you had a plan for cleaning the kitchen and the bathroom, you need a plan for cleaning any other room in your home. So have a plan in mind before you start cleaning. Which room will be first? The room nearest to you! Start by dusting the first thing that is nearest to the door inside that room. Eliminate as much walking as possible. Walking does not accomplish anything but will make you lose energy and time. Remember to work in sections. Top to bottom, just like we did in the kitchen.

DUSTING – Use two hands as much as possible. Always spray your feather dusters with dusting spray before using them. You may need to spray them only once per room or a few times per room, depending on the area you live in. If your home is in a dead end street with very little traffic, you will probably spray it less than a person who lives with two cats and a dog on the main drag.

POLISHING – Use furniture polish on your furniture only once a month or even less if possible. Not only does it take a lot longer to dust, but furniture polish builds up. It is not necessary to use a furniture polish every time. To convince yourself, try cleaning one piece of furniture with and another without furniture polish for a couple of months and you will see that it is absolutely not necessary to use a furniture polish every time. Of course, if you have little children and fingerprints are all over the place, it is difficult not to use furniture polish, but you get the idea.

MIRRORS, GLASS – Spray a mirror, the glass top of a coffee table, or glass sliding doors with sudsless ammonia and wipe with paper towels. If you have food stuck to a coffee table, loosen it with a damp sponge, then spray and wipe.

TV, VCR, AND OTHER APPLIANCES – I prefer not to use feather dusters on TVs, VCRs, and other appliances in plastic or metal cases, because it's too easy to push dust inside the vents. There are two options: a computer dust spray or a damp sponge. I like the sponge—it's cheaper and it's one less extra thing to carry. Make sure the sponge is damp, **not wet**, because water drops can cause damage inside an appliance.

WINDOW BLINDS – To keep them clean, all you need to do is use feather dusters. This way you will basically prevent dust from settling on the blinds. Trust me, they will always look clean if you lightly dust them once a month. My blinds look like new and they are eight years old. I've never had to wash them, but I always dust them, just like any other piece of furniture. However, if your blinds are less fortunate than mine and need a thorough cleaning, you have two choices:

1. You may wash them and keep them clean. I think that after all that hard work, you will be ambitious to dust them so you will not have to go through that again; or

2. Replace them. I mean it sincerely. These days, window blinds are very cheap, especially if on sale. If you consider how much time and effort you will

spend cleaning your blinds and compare it to the amount of money you will have to spend to replace them with brand new ones, you might be surprised to find out that it is cheaper to replace them than to clean them.

Here is how to clean your window blinds most efficiently. Take them **all** off and bring them to the bathroom. Fill the tub with hot water, **then** add dishwashing detergent. (If you add detergent while the tub is filling up, you will have a lot of bubbles, which you should try to avoid as bubbles make it harder to work). Always wear heavy rubber gloves, because you will definitely cut yourself no matter how careful you are. Your goal should be to concentrate on your work not on your hands if you want to speed up the process.

Spread a heavy towel on the bottom of the tub to prevent it from getting scratched and chipped by the blinds. Then put one blind in the tub. Spread out one part of it (because the tub is not wide enough to spread the whole blind), and with a scrubby sponge, clean it from side to side. After a short time, you will not even be able to see what you are doing because the water will no longer be clear. That's OK, as long as you do not miss any strips. Push the clean part up and now clean the next and the next and the next until the whole blind is done. Take it out and put another one in. When all of them are done, drain that filthy water, rinse the tub, rinse the towel, refill the tub with clean water, and put the towel back in the tub. Now rinse the blinds one by one. Drain the water again, rinse the towel and spread it on the bottom of the tub. Take one blind at a time and stand it up on its edge. Spread it as wide as possible for the quickest air drying, and lean it up against the wall. Repeat this with every blind, leaning it on a previous one. When dry, hang them up and look. If you see that you missed a spot (and I am sure you will), just take a sponge with a cleaning solution on it and wipe. This is the quickest way to clean blinds, GUARANTEED!!!

You might want to find a professional who cleans window blinds. Check stores that sell custom made blinds. Many of them will charge you $3.00 on average for each window blind.

AS YOU DUST, TRY TO READY the room for vacuuming. By this, I mean do everything now so you'll be able to vacuum without stopping. Move the chair away from the corner for easier access (make sure you move it the right way; if you move it the wrong way you will have to move it twice). This means move it in the direction you'll vacuum, otherwise the chair will get in your way before you even get to the hard-to-reach area. Move the plant stand, the magazine rack, the floor lamp the same direction. Do not get carried away and move heavy pieces of furniture; not only can you hurt yourself but it is not good for furniture to be moved often. Moving or lifting weakens it.

Never jump from one piece of furniture to the other side of the room. Always go to the very next piece, maybe even dusting a baseboard while you go. It is a tremendous waste of time if you walk through the house to clean all mirrors, then go back to dust everything with furniture polish. The larger the home, the greater the waste of time. THIS is where the efficiency belt is especially valuable. It allows you to use both hands, you avoid bending to put down or pick up cleaning products, you do not forget them anywhere, you do not spill anything... and best of all, you have both hands free to use for cleaning at all times!

Use a damp sponge to quickly wipe a leather couch or easy chair if it's covered with crumbs or pet hair. For thorough cleaning (as an extra project), use the small brush attachment of your vacuum cleaner. The bigger the brush, the weaker the suction – keep that in mind.

Now, vacuum all of the rooms without stopping and without replugging the vacuum. (Remember to plug the vacuum cleaner in one central location, like the hallway). Start vacuuming wherever you are. Vacuum part of the hallway, then the nearest room. I like to vacuum my rooms in, then to the side, then to the middle, then out of the room (see diagram). This way there are no footprints on the carpet when I finish. Looks great! As you vacuum, move back the chair, the magazine rack, the plant stand, etc., while you are backing out of the room. Finished!

Dining Room

Dust this room the same way as the rest of the rooms on this level. When dusting, move chairs away from the table about two feet. Vacuum one part of the carpet, push the chair back, vacuum the second part, push the chair back, and so on. Or pull only one chair away from the table when dusting. Later, when vacuuming, do that part first (of course, with your good planning this will be the most convenient area to start vacuuming), push the second chair into the first chair's spot, vacuum the second area, push the third chair into the second chair's spot, and continue to rotate them. Not only do you only move each chair once, but by rotating them you use all of them. We all like a particular spot at the table, so this will help you to use all chairs evenly. Same spot, different chair!

Vacuum one room, then part of the hallway, then the next room and so on. This way you will not create a project of vacuuming the hallway. It will be just a transitional area to deal with. If you start with the

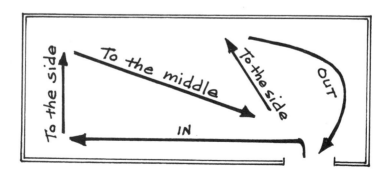

farthest room along a hallway, there will be no foot-prints on the hallway carpet when you finish. As you vacuum the area, push back what you pulled away while dusting. It can be a chair, a small corner or coffee table, a door mat....

If you empty trash bins, do not walk from where you are to the place where trash should end up. Just tie the bag securely and toss it towards the door. If you aren't sure that the bag will hold up, use a double bag. When you make your full circle dusting, toss the trash bag into the hallway and leave it there for now. Clean the next room and do the same with the trash. When you finish cleaning, you will end up with a few trash bags in the hallway. Only then pick them up and bring them where they belong. If you have trash bags on the second floor and still have to do some cleaning, do not leave your work place until totally done. Meanwhile, you can just kick them downstairs for the time being, closer to where they belong. To save time, keep the same amount of trash bags at the bottom of each waste basket. When you take trash out, use one of the bags. When you use the last one in one basket, that means it's time to replace them all. One trip, one time.

WARNING: I would not be too ambitious about kicking a bag full of diapers unless it is in a double or triple bag. Anything else is OK.

A Few Useful Tips:

WALLS

1. To dust a wall, use a dust mop sprayed with dusting spray. Work from top to bottom. Make sure there is nothing on top of furniture that can be knocked off.

2. Fingerprints or crayons on walls: Use a scrubby sponge with a bit of baking soda.

3. To clean grease from wallpaper: Apply a paste of cornstarch and water. Put a coat of it as heavy as possible on the stain. Let dry. Brush off. Repeat if needed.

LOUVERED DOORS – Use a paint brush sprayed with furniture polish or dusting spray. Use a paint brush dipped in a mild cleaner if wood is painted. Then wipe.

HARDWOOD FLOORS usually have two kinds of finish: polyurethane or satin finish. Polyurethane usually looks very shiny and you can see a layer that prevents you from touching actual floorboard. These floors are easier to care for. All you need is a dust mop sprayed with a dusting spray (without wax to prevent slippery areas). If you see spills or stains, wipe them up with a damp sponge or cloth. You can wash these floors because water will not get in contact with the wood (which can cause damage), but it definitely will make the floor dull with time.

If the wood has a satin finish, you should not wash it because water will get in contact with the wooden boards and damage the floor. Again, the best way to clean it is to use a dust mop and damp sponge for spot cleaning of stains or spills. Wax the satin finish floor twice a year. A good way to test if the floor needs to be waxed is to put a drop of water on the floor. If it stays as a round drop, it is not yet time to wax. If the drop spreads, it is time to wax the floor.

NOTE: When spreading wax around the floor, never get too close to the edge. The buffing machine can't get all the way to the wall. If wax spreads all the way to the wall, you'll have to manually buff it on your hands and knees. I don't think you would want to do that.

A few more tips for satin finish floors:

1. To get rid of scratches, use a steel wool ball dipped in floor wax.

2. To get rid of heel marks, use a dry steel wool ball or pencil eraser.

3. If your hardwood floor squeaks, sprinkle with talcum powder between the boards at the squeaky spot (applicable only to hardwood floors with satin finish).

LINOLEUM FLOORS

1. To remove crayon marks, use a soapless steel wool ball or a bit of silver cleaner on a rag.

2. To remove heel scuffs, use a dry steel wool ball. If the scuff does not go away, use a cleaner on a steel wool ball. Any cleaner without ammonia is good.

VINYL FLOORS

To remove stubborn stains, use full-strength bleach. Rinse immediately and thoroughly. It is easier than you can imagine. NOTE: Try on a hidden area first. Bleach may whiten the floor a bit. It depends on the quality of your floor covering.

CARPET

1. *Fresh stains:* Blot as much as possible first. Then pour a bit of club soda on the spot and rub with a stiff brush. Blot as much as possible. Let it dry. If soaked in deep, use a hairdryer to dry it and prevent mold.

2. *Candle wax:* Cover the stain with a piece of construction paper, paper towel, or brown paper bag. Put a hot iron over the spot to melt the wax. The paper will absorb the wax. Repeat if needed.

3. *Chewing gum:* Use an ice cube to make it brittle, then just peel it off.

4. *Most kinds of glue:* Use a rag dipped in white vinegar.

5. If the corners of your area rug are curling up, it becomes a tripping hazard. Put a heavy layer of newspaper (about two inches thick) under the edge of the carpet, dampen the curling corner of the rug, and let it sit overnight. Don't do this in the day when someone can trip over it. By morning, the corner will not be curled up anymore.

To prevent it from happening again, use double-faced masking tape on all four edges. It will not damage the rug or the floor. If your area rug is on top of carpet you can sew it on. It will always stay put.

FURNITURE:
  WOOD

1. To cover minor scratches on furniture, use the meat of a walnut (without the skin) and rub the scratch. For thicker scratches, use a shoe polish or crayon to match the color. Use a generous amount, then buff.

2. To remove water marks, rub the spot with a rag sprinkled with ammonia, or use a paste of mayonnaise and cigarette ashes, or even toothpaste. One of these should work. Do not use ammonia on any glossy-finished furniture. If you apply a coat of paste wax at least twice a year, you will prevent water stains.

3. To remove candle wax, use a hairdryer to soften it and blot with a piece of paper towel, construction paper, or brown paper bag. Or use a plastic putty knife and scrape, if the surface is flat. Do not use a metal putty knife – it can scratch and damage the surface.

4. Twice a year, oil all of your wood furniture. Make sure you follow the directions.

FABRIC

To remove grease stains, sprinkle generously with cornstarch. Rub it in. Let sit for about 15 to 20 minutes to absorb as much as possible, then brush the rest away. Repeat if needed.

GLASS SURFACES

To remove small scratches from a glass surface, rub it with toothpaste.

WICKER

1. To clean wicker furniture, use a paint brush. It gets into every corner. Clean it regularly. If you wait until it looks dirty, you'll never get it to really look clean again.

2. To wash wicker furniture, use warm water mixed with salt. It will keep it white.

3. Do not let wicker furniture freeze or it will crack and split.

My Top Ten Household Tips

1. LAUNDRY: Do not wash clothes when cleaning. The time and energy spent on sorting, loading, drying, hanging, and putting away clothes will greatly diminish the speed and effectiveness of your cleaning. You will forget that the focus is on cleaning, not laundry. Count how many times you will go up and down. You will spend the whole day cleaning and not accomplish

much, yet feel pretty tired! You can easily lose an hour on three loads and end up with a job unfinished or poorly done. This is not much of an incentive for the next cleaning, which is only two weeks away (not enough time to forget).

If you must do laundry, try this: Put a load in before you start cleaning, and when you finish cleaning on one level, put that load in the dryer and a new load in the wash. When you finish cleaning completely, attend to the rest. Keep in mind that you should not deal with it any time in between, so you may want to put in towels or sheets or something that you will not worry about. Towels are good because they take so long to dry.

2. Do not water plants when cleaning because it will take valuable time, nor do you want to water plants right after cleaning – you don't want to mess up a clean home. It's best to take care of your plants today if you plan to clean tomorrow, not the other way around. If you do not take care of your plants the day before, you will have no choice but to do it on cleaning day. Plan ahead!

3. Do not change sheets while cleaning. If you have three beds to change, it can cost you half an hour. Change your sheets the night before, before you go to bed. If you change sheets after you clean, you will see all kinds of dust, feathers, and stuff falling on your freshly vacuumed floor. Plan ahead. The less work you leave for basic

cleaning, the happier you will be, and the more enthusiastically you will start your cleaning.

Remember to focus on cleaning when cleaning your home. You will start and finish in two or three hours. Cleaning is hard work, and the less time you spend doing it, the more ambitious you will be in two weeks to do it again.

4. Do not answer the phone while cleaning. This is one of the biggest mistakes people make. It is also the hardest thing to resist. When you answer the phone, you interrupt your routine, and then after sitting down, you feel how tired you are, you see how much you still have to do, and all of a sudden you do not have the strength or desire to finish. Of course, you can force yourself, but you will not work with the same ambition, speed, and quality. It's sort of like exercising – you are OK until you stop. Then it's all over. So the best thing to do is to listen to the caller's message (in case it is an emergency) but do not answer if it can wait.

5. Do not wash dishes. Put them all in the dishwasher. If some have to be washed by hand, do them after cleaning your home. Why? Because tired or not, you will do dishes, but the same does not apply to general cleaning. Or maybe better – someone else in your home will do the dishes, but I can assure you no one will do the basic cleaning for you. Not today, not tomorrow, not in a month.

6. Do not listen to the radio or TV. It is a tremendous distraction. When you clean, your mind should be ahead of your hands, and if your mind is with the radio, you will slow down, not speed up – guaranteed! TV is even worse. You not only listen but also keep an eye on it, so you are even more distracted, and worse, you are not in a hurry to leave the room. On the other hand, if you are in a miserable mood and still willing to clean, the radio might help you to get through the job. You'll be slower than usual, but at least you will finish. Or maybe you will finish on time, but the quality will not be there. The bottom line is that radio and TV are no good while cleaning.

7. If your family is home, you will be working slower. You might be able to involve your family – maybe your spouse can do the laundry, your kids can pick up their toys off the floor (or else they will become yours).... If you ask family for help, do not give them assignments that will take too long – either they will not finish by the time you reach the area or they will not do it right. Of course, there are exceptions, but you know the ability of your helpers, so do not overload them. Who knows? You might even get some help.

   If you don't get them involved in cleaning, they will get in your way. The solution is simple – stay away from me! If your home has two levels, make them go up when you are cleaning downstairs. When you go up, they go down. No discussions, no talking, no interruptions, no kids coming over to play during these two hours. You are the priority at this time (don't you wish to be a priority more often?). Another thing you might do is to send your family out food shopping or to the movies. But beware – they might spend more than you will save by not hiring professional cleaning help!!!

8. Do not spend all your energy and time cleaning the kitchen. You still have the whole house to clean. That means don't open the mail, just put an elastic band over all of the envelopes so they are in one place and look neat. When you finish cleaning, sit down and open all of it, but not now.

9. Do not rearrange closets, shelves, cabinets... even as an extra project. It will take three times longer than you think – GUARANTEED!!!

10. Do not polish shoes, do not let your dog in or out, do not sew buttons, do not sort laundry, do not straighten up your office papers (well, maybe you should let the dog out).

11. Do not put toys back together. Just get them off the floor. I recommend bringing with you a black garbage bag (think ahead) and dumping all toys in it when cleaning. Kids will assemble them as needed later. Save your time and energy.

CHAPTER 3
Spring Cleaning

What is Spring Cleaning?

We often hear the term "Spring Cleaning." To us it means a heavy-duty monster of a job, something we are not looking forward to, and something that will take an incredible amount of time and/or money. Most of us do not have the time, money, or desire to do it, and spring cleaning becomes something that can wait until later. So we live with a dream that some day we will find the time and inclination to do it. Fat chance!

Yes, some of us do spring cleaning occasionally. And then we talk about it until next time. After all, we worked so long and so hard.

Relax. Spring cleaning is a term that comes from the old days when people heated their homes with coal, which would cover everything inside a home with dust and soot in the winter. In spring, when windows were open at last, people could not wait for the first opportunity to clean their homes and get some fresh air. So they did a "Spring Cleaning." It was pretty much a necessity.

Our lives are rather hectic. Today we have larger homes, less help, less time, kids that need driving to karate, dance, music, and everything else that their little hearts desire. But wait, that's not all. We need to find time to go with them to the toy store to buy them another not needed toy which later we will have to pick up from the floor to be able to clean. No wonder we are so busy that we do not have time to rest, never mind clean!

There should not be any spring cleaning to speak of unless you have a coal stove (which isn't nearly as messy as it was in the old days). Even then it is not much work to keep it clean. It is a good idea to hang a small hand vacuum cleaner on the wall to pick up spilled ashes or dirt from around the stove before it spreads through the house. Make sure you hang it far enough away from the stove so it won't suffer heat damage and won't be in the way when you're cleaning the stove. Before loading and unloading your coal stove, always put a newspaper down to catch anything that falls out. If you are considering buying a coal stove, buy one that has an ash drawer, so you can just slide the drawer out and dump the ashes. It helps if the surface around and under the stove is smooth – it makes it harder for the debris to get stuck.

For cleaning anything other than a wood or coal stove, you do not need to wait until a spring cleaning. All you need is an extensive list of extra work. Remember we were talking about a list of extra work before? Then I suggested making it short and reasonable, not to list things like cleaning your basement. Now you can make that list as extensive as you wish. Keep in mind that The Cleaning Fairy will not come to do it for you. YOU will have to do it yourself, so think before writing a project on the list. On the other hand, you can always cut back when you have enough. No one will judge you. You can do all of it, or as much of it as you can handle at one time. That can be a day or a weekend (some great way to spend a weekend!), or do as much as possible here and there through the month. May or June are good times, because it is warm enough to open windows yet not too hot.

Whatever you decide has to be planned out and you should commit yourself to doing it. If you can't commit to certain dates and certain amounts of work, don't even start – you will be disappointed. It will be best for you to leave it as a dream – someday you will have time to do it. And I hope you will. If you do a bit of extra work now and then during your basic cleaning, or if you choose one day per month for extras only, you will minimize your spring cleaning to a point that it will be a very small and easily managed job. It will be a pleasure to do just a bit and call it a spring cleaning.

Do not use the term "Spring Cleaning" as an excuse to put off all or most of your extra cleaning projects. This is a guarantee that your home will never have a chance to be totally clean. The toilet bowl should never be a spring cleaning project!

"Spring Cleaning" usually involves cleaning areas that aren't often used or are out of the way and not often seen. We think if such an area is dirty, it does not affect us, so we put it off. But please, clean – even the unseen.

"Spring Cleaning" jobs can include moving heavy pieces of furniture so you can get behind and underneath them to clean the wall and baseboard. Make sure you take all drawers out. Not only is it easier to move furniture to get to these places, but you can also vacuum inside. Yes, it gets dusty there too. It can include moving a bed so you can clean the baseboard and carpet behind the headboard. On your basic cleaning day, you might be able to reach some of it with the extension hose but to do a perfect job you need to move it. And you need to do a perfect job not only because it looks good, but mainly because you will breathe in all that dust that accumulates behind the headboard. It is not healthy and can cause dust allergies.

Another area for "Spring Cleaning" is between and behind the washer and dryer, refrigerator, stove, books.... Clean all your artificial flowers.... If you do not want to clean it – get rid of it! It certainly will not look pretty and will not decorate your home if it is covered with dust and cobwebs.

Just like with basic cleaning, you need to have all your supplies with you to eliminate wasting time spent picking them up, putting them down, walking back and forth to get them, or simply misplacing them. And just like with basic cleaning, you should clean from top to bottom, section by section, and do not leave the spot until all is done there. Then move on to a new project.

A summary for "Spring Cleaning":

1. Make an extensive list of what to do so you can see what is needed.

2. Make sure you have all the supplies you need.

3. Make sure you know how to clean all of what you set out to do.

4. Put down dates when you can do it. Commit yourself to these dates.

Where Do I Start?

Before you start a Spring Cleaning (I will nag you to death about this), plan your work. Know where you need to start, how you will proceed, and where you will finish. Then get ready – decide what you will need for this job to make it go as easily and smoothly as possible. Get all cleaning supplies (do not be afraid to use stronger stuff than usual because it will help you to do the work faster and will not do damage because you will use it so seldom), heavy duty rubber gloves, mop, broom, trash bags, boxes, brushes.... Do everything you have to do so that you will not have excuses for stopping. Then go for it!

WASHING WALLS

1. Wallpaper: If it is washable, use a mild detergent to wash it with the least amount of water. I do not mean a little bit in the bucket, I mean squeeze out the sponge as much as you can so the wallpaper will not be soaked. Never wet the edges of wallpaper seams. They will warp and ruin the look of the wallpaper. However, if that happens, use a glue stick first. If that is not enough, use clear nail polish to seal the seam. Make sure the wallpaper is totally dry before gluing edges back in place. If the wallpaper is

not washable, use erasers or artgum squares, available in stationery or art supply stores.

2. Paneling: You may wash it with a mind detergent (try not to overwet it). You can also use a dust mop (with a clean refill). Spray generously with a no-wax dusting spray and wipe the wall. It will also give it shine.

3. Painted walls: If washable, use any mild cleaner. If not washable, try an eraser (as described above), a damp (not wet) sponge, or even a mop to wipe off fingerprints and dirt. Use the same mop that you would use to wash the floor, only replace the sponge. Make sure it is damp, but not wet.

4. If you have small cracks in walls, cover them with toothpaste. It does a great job.

5. If you need to move furniture (it is not a must), always empty it first. Not only will it be easier to move and prevent injury, but it is easier on furniture (moving furniture makes it wobbly). If you use a dust mop, you might not need to move a large piece of furniture because a long handle allows you to reach pretty much everywhere.

WINDOWS

Think long and hard before committing yourself to washing windows, especially if you have to climb a ladder to do it. Evaluate how long it will take you to do it, and how much money you will save by doing it yourself. Only then, if you think it is worth it, should you go ahead and do it. Here is how:

Take a bucket of water (any temperature you like), add to it some ammonia (about one cup per gallon), and wash your window with the sponge. When the dirt is off, just spray with your favorite glass cleaner and wipe with a paper towel. This is the quickest way to wash a dirty window.

If you choose to hire help, decide what is more important to you – the spotless window (which will be not so spotless in a week) or a few dollars in your pocket. You can guess my opinion! If you have a lot of windows as I do, you can save at least $10-$15 dollars by going through the yellow pages to find the cheapest company. By the way, when you do find someone who is cheaper, you will not have to find him again. Next year may involve just a couple of phone calls to reassure yourself of the competitive price.

You might want to brush your screens during a spring cleaning because when they are dusty they let dust in the house with every breeze; dusty screens also let less light through. This job is easy. You can take screens out from the inside, so you don't have to climb a ladder.

TO CLEAN A CHANDELIER

First, never touch a hot bulb because it can crack. That means you have to wash it during the day time. There are great cleaners on the market that you can spray generously on a chandelier and let drip dry. For that you need to cover a large area under the chandelier with something rubbery to protect the floor from drips; the best thing is a shower curtain. The problem is that these sprays are not meant for metal finishes that most chandeliers have. So before buying a spray cleaner, read the label carefully to be sure it is safe for the metal finish on your chandelier. If you aren't sure, call the company and ask. If you're still not sure that it is safe for metal parts, make sure you wipe the metal parts immediately in case any of the cleaner has dripped on them.

Another choice is to wash it manually, the old-fashioned way. It seems funny I should say this, but considering that you do it only once a year (many of us do it even less often), it is worth it to do it manually rather than damaging the metal part of the fixture. Here is how:

Cover the surface below with something soft like a blanket, because when crystals fall it will keep them from breaking. Step high enough so you can reach it easily (on a table or a ladder...) with a lot of paper towels in your pocket and a bottle of ammonia mix. Take two sheets of paper towel, spray the paper towels generously with ammonia and squeeze a few crystals of chandelier between two hands. Rub till they look clean. Clean a few more crystals next to the first ones. Go on. Do not waste your time making it perfect at the moment and do not pay attention to pieces that fall. Just concentrate on speed. When you finish, get off the ladder, turn the lights on, see if something has to be touched up and remember where it is, pick up what fell, hang it back up, touch up what you spotted, and turn the lights on again. It should be perfect now. And you only climbed the ladder twice. Not bad for once a year cleaning.

LAMP SHADES

If they are very dusty, vacuum as much as possible. If this is not enough, you can wash them in the bath tub with a cleaning solution if they are plastic, or with mild laundry detergent if they are fabric. Lay down a large towel to protect the tub from scratches. Always use a hairdryer to dry near the metal frame to prevent rust. In the future, to prevent lamp shades from getting dirty, use a two-inch wide paintbrush to clean them about once a month.

TV AND ELECTRONICS

Once a month, vacuum it all, get the dust out, and prevent it from settling inside – your TV or computer will last much longer. Use your canned-air spray (see supplies) or a paper towel and glass cleaner. If you choose the paper towel and glass cleaner, always spray the paper towel, never the screen, to prevent drips that can get inside and cause damage.

FAKE FLOWERS

You may use a thin, soft paint brush to dust them about once a month, or vacuum them (be careful, the vacuum cleaner can suck the flower off the stem), or dip them one by one in a solution of water and laundry detergent (every three months or so). Make sure your flowers are not real silk or they will be ruined. Remember that your flowers are suppose to decorate your home. If they are in a pitiful state, they are not beautiful, they are junk – get rid of them. If you choose to buy new ones, keep them looking good or do not buy artificial flowers.

Helpful Tips

1. Put a perfumed advertising insert from a magazine into any drawer to make it smell nice.

2. To remove an adhesive residue of masking or duct tape from furniture, cover the area with lemon oil or any other furniture oil and let it sit for 10-15 minutes. Then scrub gently with a nylon scrubbing pad or a dry scrubby sponge.

3. To have hangers slide easily in your closet, rub the rod with a candle. Wax makes it easy to move hangers. Candle wax is also great for sticky drawers. Rub wax along the sides and runners.

4. Can never find a piece of jewelry you are looking for? Display it. Use a picture frame: Take the glass out and replace it with felt or any other thick fabric like you see in a jewelry shop in the case. Stick your pins and pierced earrings on it. Under it attach to the wall a kids size coat rack with pegs for your chains, beads, necklaces, bracelets. It's also great for hair ribbons and bands.

5. To prevent candle wax from sticking to the bottom of a candlestick, fill the little cup with water before putting in the candle. The candle stump will pop out easily.

6. If you need to move furniture on a hardwood floor, put heavy socks or gloves on the legs to prevent scratches.

7. To clean the brick around a fireplace, use straight white vinegar and wipe dry with a sponge or towel **immediately** to prevent streaks.

CHAPTER 4

Still Need Help?
Hire a Pro

By now you probably have a pretty good idea of what it takes to clean your home. If you feel that you cannot dedicate the time, do not have the physical energy, or for whatever reason choose not to clean your home yourself, consider hiring help. I strongly recommend professional help. However, the choice is yours.

You can hire:

1. A high school kid or someone who does not clean for a living

2. A self-employed person with or without employees

3. A large cleaning company

Further in this chapter, I will explain major differences between each of the above, but first before you pick up the phone and call any company (even one referred by a friend), consider following these steps if you wish to save money.

Determine Your Needs

You need to evaluate the amount of work in your home. Yes, of course you know what needs to be done and how often, but take a closer look at your home before hiring – if you want to save money and hire intelligently. Please understand that the more work a cleaning company provides for you of course the better, but you also have to understand that they will charge **you** for every bit they do. So take a grand tour of your home as you did before, but look at your home with a different goal in mind. Create three lists:

1. The **MUST** list will be jobs that are absolutely unavoidable, like the kitchen, bathroom, master bedroom....

2. The **PREFERRED** list will be jobs that you would very much like done but, depending on the price, you might choose to eliminate or alternate, such as the spare bedroom, computer room, toy room....

3. The **EXTRA** list consists of jobs that have to be done, but not every time, like the refrigerator inside, the oven inside... pretty much the same as the list of extras you made for yourself earlier.

Now look at the whole picture. To save the most, you need to be sure that the cleaning crew will have to clean the least **you** can get away with. Everything on the "must list" will have to be cleaned by the cleaning company and probably most things on the "preferred list." But how often? You can hire someone to clean the whole house bi-weekly, and on the off weeks you can clean the bathroom yourself. Or you can have the whole house cleaned one week, and the next time have them clean just the downstairs, which usually needs cleaning more often than the bedrooms upstairs. Save half price every other time. Think hard, think twice, then make a decision you will not regret.

For extra projects, you will likely have to pay extra money. Usually a cleaning company will charge you an extra few dollars to clean something extra, but you can offer them a switch. Say: "Can you clean inside the fridge today and skip a kid's bedroom?" This way it will not cost you any actual cash. Some companies will just clean it for the sake of having a satisfied customer, but there are fewer and fewer of them. Don't be surprised if they ask for extra money.

You can hire someone to clean weekly, bi-weekly (more common), every three weeks, or even monthly. It is for **you** to decide. Do not ask how often they think your home should be cleaned. As honest as they will be, they will not know. They do not know your family, your habits, and your standards. Only you can answer that question. Do not fall for their suggestion to try it every week and then cut down if it is too much. Your house can never be too clean and you will end up paying more than you need.

Never say to a cleaning company that you are very fussy. They will charge you a higher fee because they will expect to do more work for you. You are, in fact, helping them to justify a higher price.

Do not confuse the quality of work with the quantity of work. Every cleaning company should provide top quality work for every job they do, but if you ask them to do more work, it will cost you more.

So now you know exactly what you need them to do for you and how often.

Per Hour or Per Job

Now you need to decide if you need someone who will charge per hour or per job. These days, very few companies will agree to charge per hour, because if the same job is done every time, the same amount of money should be paid. Cleaning people improve their speed when they clean the same home again and again. In many other jobs, employees get a raise for doing work faster, but in cleaning the opposite is true if paid per hour – less time equals less money. So cleaning people more often will charge per job.

As for you, if you always have the same amount of work, it should not make a difference. In fact, it is better for you this way too – you know exactly how much work will be done and how much it will cost you, and you will not have to watch the clock. If you have different work for a cleaning company every time they come, then you may have to put effort into finding someone who will charge per hour.

Self-Employed or Large Company

Now you need to decide if you prefer a very small company (two or three employees), or a self-employed person, or a high school kid, or a large company to work for you. Here are the differences:

INSURANCE – There are two policies you should be concerned with: liability, which covers damages and injuries to you on your property; and bonding, which covers theft by employees.

A large company will probably carry both types of insurance. Small companies, and especially self-employed people might not be able to afford insurance, which can be well over a thousand dollars per year. That's a lot of homes to clean for one small company. A high school kid will not have insurance coverage. We hire high school kids without insurance to babysit our children, so maybe it's okay to trust them with our floors and bathrooms. It's a tough call.

You decide how important insurance is for you. For me, insurance is important. Whenever I hire a plumber, carpenter, or anyone to work in my house, I always check that his or her insurance is up to date. If it is important for you too, then you can ask if a company has insurance coverage. If "Yes," you can ask for a "certificate of insurance" to be mailed to you. This is an official statement from an insurance company that a policy exists. They will also notify you in the case of a change in the policy. Insurance companies send these certificates every day.

The cleaning company that has insurance coverage will think that you appreciate their extra effort. You will know the name of the insurance company, the expiration date (so you can check if the policy has been renewed), and the amount of coverage. More importantly, if damages occur, you will know where to make a claim.

In case you ever have a claim, make sure you have adequate proof of value. Receipts, pictures (before and after), and appraisals (for valuable antiques and jewelry) will all back you up. (It's probably a good idea to keep a copy of all this at a friend or relative's house in case of fire). Hold on to any damaged items until the case is settled.

Don't let a cleaning person who damages something get away with just saying "Sorry!" If you already know the insurance carrier, it will be easier to claim damages.

REFERENCES – Always ask for a reference, but bear in mind what the reference really tells you. A reference on a large company might not be on the same cleaning crew that will come to you. What good is it? You might get a reference on the same supervisor, but a different crew. Again what good is the reference? There usually is high turnover in a large company. The crew you get a reference on might not be the same people who are cleaning your home next week.

For a self-employed person, on the other hand, references are very easy to get. Every self-employed person will give you his or her clients' names for references. Pay attention to whether the cleaner has the permission of a client to give out a phone number. If you would not like your phone number given out, make sure you say so.

NOTE: If the only references you get are from clients who have been using this self-employed person's services for only two or three months, and the company has been in business for three years or longer, I would wonder why.

If you happen to come across a person who is totally new to the cleaning business and without references, it is not necessary to reject him. You can ask for references from a previous job. Although no one will tell you much about his quality of cleaning, you will learn about his dedication, honesty, and reliability.

This reference is important because you let this person into your home where you live and have everything you own. References would not be that important if you hired someone to cut the grass outside your home, but for inside your home it is critical. As for the cleaning itself, give her a chance and you can judge for yourself. Remember, every person has different standards. What is good for one might not be good enough for the other.

Another thing to keep in mind with references is that the person giving the reference is in a funny position. She can jeopardize her relationship with a cleaning person if she doesn't give a good reference and can cause the cleaning person to lose a client. The best thing to do is to use your judgment and perhaps give this person a chance. People go into business to make a living. Their goal is to please customers. They cannot have a business without you and without a good reputation. These people work for themselves, not for a company, and that changes the whole picture. Their attitude is to please you – a client.

Often a self-employed person will follow your lead, using supplies you like, and cleaning some things a different way because you prefer it that way. It is harder with a large company. They might say, "This is our rule, these are the supplies we use...." It is much harder for them to adapt to your preferences because they work on a much larger scale.

As for a high school kid, you probably know your neighbor's kid very well. He might have even babysat for your baby. He can be trusted, but will definitely need your guidance in cleaning – what exactly needs to be done, what cleaning products to use (and you must provide them). This kid will most likely do everything you ask for, but **you** must watch the clock. High school kids will not be as efficient as a professional and of course will not be insured. But they will definitely charge much less.

ADS – Do not jump on ads that say "twenty years of experience." It certainly is great to have someone with so much experience to come and clean your home, but do you really think that the person who started the business twenty years ago will actually come and clean your house? Probably not. Most like-ly, someone who was hired three month ago will come, someone who does not even own the business. When you get an estimate and that person says proudly that she has been in business for twenty years, that certainly implies that she knows the business well, knows the right supplies to use, and will mix commercial cleaning products safely. (This is very important because the wrong proportions can cause damage. What is even worse is that damage might not be noticeable until months later. This company may not even be cleaning for you any longer. Yet the paint is chipping, the finish is getting duller....) Ask if this person will clean your home personally or at least come into your home to supervise the crew. The chances are very slim. Often the owner is busy with other aspects of running her business (and there is plenty to do as in any other business, believe me).

Someone who is very new to the housecleaning business might not know all of the latest cleaning solutions and all of the best techniques, but this person will be the most dedicated. **For one**, the beginner is not in a position to lose a client so he/she will be very reasonable with price and the amount of work he/she will do, **and two**, he/she will try very hard to please. This person will never tell you, "This is our policy, we do it only this way, we use only these supplies, this is the only day I can come...." In other words, the new person will be much more accommodating. These people are building a business and they cannot succeed without you. The owner will be personally in touch with you, and will know your preferences, desires, and needs. This is unlikely to happen with a large company. They have to have rules and regulations for everyone to follow or there will be more exceptions to the rule than followers of the rules.

Sometimes an ad will say "so many years of combined experience." This can be deceiving. It means that every person's experience in the company is added together. It sounds like a lot of years when actually the company is much younger.

KEYS – A large company will have a system for taking care of keys. Ask how they label them. Do not permit any company to put your name, address, or phone number on the key chain. If anyone gets a hold of those keys, you and your home will be in jeopardy. This is too serious a matter to ignore. State loud and clear that you do not allow them to put any identifying marks on the key chain with your key on it.

Another important thing is not to allow anyone to make a copy of your key. If the cleaners need more than one copy of your key, they should ask you for it. It is your home and you must know how many copies of your keys are floating around.

If you do not want cleaners to have access to your home, there are some options to choose from:

1   You can ask them to come early in the morning before you go to work. This way you let them in and they pull the door shut when leaving.

2. If you have two locks on your front door, you might want to give them a key to the dead bolt lock and leave the other lock open. When they leave they can release the top lock and use the dead bolt key to lock it, so the door is properly locked when they leave.

3. You might ask them to pick up the key from a neighbor and put it on the table before they leave. This will save them the trouble of returning a key. They will also not feel that the neighbor is keeping a timer on them.

4. If you have an alarm system that you can activate without knowing a code, you can leave it

off in the morning. The cleaning person can turn it on when he or she leaves. If you can program more than one code, you can give the cleaning person his or her own code. You can even delete the code that night, as long as you remember to put it back the next time.

Go For It!

Now that you are clear on the above issues, you may call. Choose carefully whom you call. Compare apples to apples. If you choose to hire a self-employed person, call a few other self-employed people; don't call one self-employed person, one large company, and one high school kid. It has to be the same, otherwise you will not have a true estimate. I often compare it to shopping: You can buy things at a flea market, at K-Mart, or at Macy's. Prices will vary. It's the same with housecleaning.

Actual quote – Let's say you get a quote of $60.00 from one company and $65.00 from another. It does not automatically mean that the latter company is more expensive than the first. Maybe they'll provide more work. How do you find out? Ask. What will this amount of money buy? Does it include baseboards, blinds, and the bulbs above the bathroom mirror? It might be worth it to pay a bit more to get a lot more done. On the other hand, if money is an issue, you may be happier to spend less and accept the fact that it will not be perfect. It is entirely your choice and there is no right or wrong. When you show your home to the person who will do the estimate, show everything. There is a limit to how much they will charge. They are well aware of the competition and will not overcharge you. **Don't** say anything now. Just show your home and listen. When they finish and give you the estimate, then you **must** speak up.

First, ask what this estimate will include. Will they dust baseboards throughout the house, will they *clean* or *dust* (very different things) window blinds, will they clean burner plates or just wipe the stove top? You have to know exactly what will be done, because after the first cleaning they can tell you that they did not charge you for it. And if you did not ask, you cannot say that you expected it done. They are not mind readers. Now you are in a better position to ask and get some work done for no extra charge. They need you as a client. When you become a client, then it is too late to discuss your expectations.

Be reasonable. If you try to overload a pro who has a good reputation and an established business he/she may reject the job. Then you know you asked for too much. Be honest with your requests. If in a month or two, you ask for more work, you should expect to pay additional charges. If they agree to do it for free one time, don't think you can ask for more work two months later and get it free again. They might do some more work without requesting more payment, but they will drop you as soon as they get a client to replace you, if the additions become a trend. Don't let it happen to you. Discuss everything at the time of the estimate after they give you the price and tell you exactly what will be done.

Now, when all is said and the schedule is set and the price is established, ask about extra work if you feel that you want them to do it. What about cleaning inside the refrigerator or oven – will you be able to do it when I need it? A good company will never reject a customer's request, but they might not do it for free. You can always offer to trade off an every-time task for an extra job. Then you will get it done at no extra charge.

When the price is right, you might say, "It's fine, let's set the date." You might say, "It's too much for me to pay so I would like to skip that room. How much will this lower my bill? And if we skip another room also, how much will it cost me now? What if we alternate the kids' bedrooms?" Think about it. It is very easy to skip the spare bedroom or the computer room, and you can save a bundle that way. Or say, "Let's do the whole house one time, and next time only the downstairs." Or only the downstairs and bathroom upstairs (skipping the bedrooms). Get the idea? Now the price will only go down. These people want your business so they will accommodate. If you speak at the time of the estimate, it will be in your favor; if you speak after the first cleaning, they will say that they did only what they charged for. But they will be happy to adjust the amount of work and price accordingly.

So make your decision and hire help. You will enjoy your free time. I assure you it will be well worth it.

Best of luck!

Order Form

Name: _____

Address: _____

City: _____ State: _____

Zip Code: _____ Telephone: _____

Take 10% off your total purchase (merchandise only) if you order two or more items.

_____copies @ $15.99 $_____

_____belts @ $12.99 $_____

Less 10% (two or more items) $_____

Shipping: ($3.00 first item – $1.00 each add.) $_____

Total amount enclosed: **$**_____

Prices are subject to change.

Payable by Check, Postal Money Order, VISA, MasterCard, Discover or American Express

Card #: _____ Expiry: _____

Signature: _____

Send to: Jane A. Lawson
                  P.O. Box 4224, Peabody, MA 01961
                  Tel: (978) 535-7091; Fax: (617) 884-5209
                  E-mail: queenclean@bigfoot.com

Reader's Feedback

This book is the result of your feedback and requests. We would appreciate your candid evaluation of this book.

Did you find this book as helpful as you thought it would be? _____

_____

What do you want to know more about? _____

_____

_____

Other comments: _____

_____

_____

_____

Thank you for taking the time to respond. Your thoughtful consideration helps us to continue to improve.